THE
Coffee Lover's
COMPANION

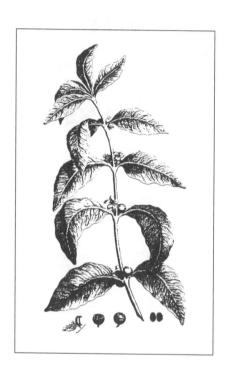

THE
Coffee Lover's
COMPANION

✧✧✧

THE ULTIMATE CONNOISSEUR'S GUIDE TO BUYING, BREWING AND ENJOYING COFFEE

Diana Rosen

With Illustrations From
The Great American Coffee and Tea Collection

A BIRCH LANE PRESS BOOK
PUBLISHED BY CAROL PUBLISHING GROUP

A Birch Lane Press Book
Published by Carol Publishing Group
Birch Lane Press is a registered trademark of
Carol Communications, Inc.

Editorial, sales and distribution, rights and permissions inquiries
should be addressed to Carol Publishing Group,
120 Enterprise Avenue, Secaucus, N.J. 07094

In Canada: Canadian Manda Group, One Atlantic Avenue, Suite 105,
Toronto, Ontario M6K 3E7

Carol Publishing books may be purchased in bulk
at special discounts for sales promotion, fund-raising,
or educational purposes. Special editions can be created to
specifications. For details, contact Special Sales Department,
120 Enterprise Avenue, Secaucus, N.J. 07094.

Manufactured in the United States of America
10 9 8 7 6 5 4 3 2 1

Library of Congress Cataloging-in-Publication Data
Rosen, Diana.
    The coffee lover's companion : the ultimate connoisseur's guide to buying,
brewing, and enjoying coffee / Diana Rosen : with illustrations from the
great American coffee and tea collection.
        p.   cm.
    "A Birch Lane Press book."
    Includes bibliographical references.
    ISBN 1-55972-368-8 (hardcover)
    1. Coffee. 2. Coffee brewing. I. Title.
TX415.R68   1997
641.3'373—dc21

96-37638
CIP

Contents

INTRODUCTION

What is it about coffee that brings out conviviality even in the most reserved? Some allege that it is the Devil's drink, exciting the blood and causing the mind to engage in the polemics of politics. Others might view the "black broth" of the ancient Spartans as a dangerously stimulating drink that loosens the tongues, the spirits, and yes, even the morals of those who savor its hot, thick, satiny liquor and breathe in its intoxicating aroma.

"Coffee should be black as hell, strong as death, and sweet as love," the ancient Turks said. However one describes coffee, it's the fuel of highly charged sociability.

It is true that coffee's aroma has an awesome power to linger, even permeate; its taste supersedes all others.

While certainly millions savor coffee while alone—in the car, at their desks, at the kitchen table—it is much more frequently the drink of hospitality among friends. From its earliest recorded history, coffee has been the drink of community, always available at every shop in the noisy bustling bazaars of the Middle East; offered to dispel sleepiness among the devoted reciting meditations in Moslem mosques or at Sufi *dhikrs* (meetings). Coffee has been the drink of choice for the European businessman, intellectual, and, more often, the layabout, offering opinions while reading the daily newspapers in coffeehouses throughout Europe. Ever since that infamous Boston "incident," coffee has decidedly been the American beverage of choice.

In the United States in particular, much has changed in the last twenty years; coffee has become a supremely elegant and sophisticated beverage, no longer relegated to the greasy spoon where a good cup of joe was the fuel for a nation. Espresso has become de rigueur for Generations X, Y, and Z, and coffee "drinks" are sipped by "fitness buffs" who blithely ignore the four hundred or more calories in each frothy cup. (Those who order nonfat, hold-the-this-and-that don't really want good coffee, they want a sweetened beige drink with chocolate curls on top.)

Despite the fashion for overroasting and the proliferation of cutesy coffee drinks, those of us who really love both the aroma and the full-mouth ecstasy of a beautifully made cup of coffee can now enjoy an even greater selection of excellent beans. Thanks are due to the proliferation of high-quality coffee merchants who have taken the time and energy to seek out the best beans and coffee accoutrements to make your at-home cup as wonderful as any you can experience in a coffeehouse, restaurant, or retail coffee shop.

Coffeehouses have had their ups and downs in popularity but are definitely on the upswing once again. In the twenties, especially in Europe, the coffeehouse was the salon of arts and letters and a place for fermenting political opinion. Those coffee salons lost much of their glamour, and many of their customers, when World War II began. In the fifties, the Beat Generation, both in the United States and Europe, created a new audience for the coffeehouse, which was resuscitated with the familiar great coffee, good jazz, and debatable poetry. Next came the Pepsi Generation, and coffee fizzled for a while until specialty coffees took hold.

The appeal of specialty coffees came at a time when many people were looking for a stimulant to replace recreational drugs and alcohol. Alcohol consumption has decreased as Americans' awareness of health issues has increased. The positive impact of the Twelve Step movement has turned more people on to the stimulating effect of coffee and its incredible variety, in both its hot and iced form. Now, nearly everyone's lexicon includes *caffè latte*, *café con leche*, and *café au lait*. Coffee isn't just straight black joe, it's one helluva lotta fun!

Ironically, the frantic pace of most people's lives has not always persuaded them to drink coffee at home. It is as if people need to give themselves permission to relax. Or perhaps they think it's more acceptable to spend time in a coffeehouse than at home with a freshly brewed espresso.

Another reason some people prefer coffee at the coffeehouse is that they don't know how to make a great cup at home. This is most likely due to the coffee-making machinery more than the bean. Most coffee blenders prefer the French plunge pot or the vacuum pot. The reason for each preference is the same: Each brews in four minutes, provides a smooth, clean, rich cup, and is easy to take anywhere. For those who simply cannot live without the convenience of an electric coffeepot, the choice most definitely is the at-home version of the commercial Bunn-o-Matic.

The grind of the bean is critical to creating a perfect cup. It's important to remember that the finer the grind, the less time it takes to brew, and the coarser the grind, the more time it takes to brew. It is difficult to have a smooth brew without uniformly ground coffee. No brewing cycle should ever be longer than eight minutes. The ideal for most coffee grinds is four minutes, no matter what kind of brewer you have. The objective is to get the most flavor extracted out of the grounds without the bitterness, that "off" taste that is, in truth, a natural part of coffee. It's also very critical to use good water. What is in the water is in the coffee.

Coffee blenders I spoke with differed about quantity of water and coffee. One even suggested using equal amounts of coffee and water for an ultrastrong brew; another suggested one rounded tablespoon of coffee per six ounces of water; others suggested two level tablespoons per six ounces of water.

What's a coffee novice to think? Think for himself, of course. Use your taste buds as a guide. Start off with two level tablespoons per six ounces of water and adjust according to your own taste. It is much easier to dilute the brew, because you certainly cannot make a weak brew stronger after the fact.

It is important to buy the product, not the marketing. You, as the consumer, need to trust your own taste buds; you are in charge. Your palate will find its way through the maze of choices and hyperbole. Discover what you like by sampling coffees for yourself, instead of waiting for someone else's opinion to determine what you should like. Compare, experiment, and in the process, you will find great joy and satisfaction in many a fine cup.

Today more than ever before, there is a considerable disparity between quality and price. More players are in the coffee game, and more poor-quality coffee is being palmed off as good-quality coffee, yet the demand for exceptional coffee is greater than ever. Growers, in an effort to meet the demand, have developed hybrid coffee plants that give considerably higher production but not necessarily a higher-quality bean. Mixing high- and low-quality beans to increase the volume in the cup is not uncommon. Although quality has definitely gone way up in the last ten years, all this change makes for a tremendous challenge for the coffee buyer. She must now spend more time cupping (tasting) more coffees just to get the minimum requirements for her company or shop. Her dedicated efforts, though, mean you can still get the best. A first step for you is to find that good, ethical coffee merchant.

How do you become educated? You ask a lot of questions of the coffee merchant and, certainly at first, go from merchant to merchant seeking out the best beans. No reputable coffee merchant would ever deter you in your quest. In fact, if they don't have something, they'll most likely refer you to someone who does. Coffee is a beverage of nuance, with slight differences in roasting making a completely different cup. Different roasters in the same shop can end up with slightly different results. Crops differ from year to year, and all the other factors related to any food product come into play in the final bean. It takes time to become learned about coffee, but broad-based shopping will give you the good foundation you need. Best of all, it's a relatively low-cost experiment and it's fun!

What are the great coffees today? Jamaica Blue Mountain is more marketing than reality, although the more recent crops have been quite fine. One of my favorites, New

Guinea, has often been lumped with Indonesian, but is finally coming into its own. Its sweet, heavy body is proof that it's not just any old bean, it is arabica at its finest. Among the reliable beans at your coffee merchant, try the selections from Sumatra and the other Indonesian favorite beans from the archipelago islands: Sumatra, Celebes, Ankola, and Mandheling. For those with a palate for more "acidic" beans, try Kenya AA, the number-one choice of most coffee merchants with whom I talked.

The "centrals," those from Central American countries, continue to astonish both for their completeness and for their ability to make the most modest bean perk up: Costa Rica in particular, but true Guatemala Antiguas are at the top of everyone's list. Some blenders touted their own blends, and some simply preferred the taste of blended coffees over straight brews. This is a great example of how taste buds and palate preferences differ. If they vary for the blenders, it stands to reason that your selections can vary from those of your friends. The coffee you buy should have what you like in it, not what someone said you should like. After all, the only person drinking that cup is you.

The first "gourmet" coffee I ever had was Colombia Supremo, which a coffee fiend I knew insisted was the only bean to use. I later found out he never cooked with garlic, so I ceased to rely on his opinion for anything. I do credit him that Colombia Supremo is a damn fine everyday coffee, as is its sister, Colombia Excelso. Unfortunately, Colombian coffee is perceived to be greater than its taste would reveal, thanks mostly to a very long-term, prolific advertising campaign from canned-coffee companies who have tried to impress upon the American public that "mountain-grown" Colombian is the finest in the world. I beg to differ. I want so much to say that Hawaiian Kona coffee is fabulous, but it's just too mild for my taste, but if you're sipping it on Maui with your beloved, it suddenly becomes the most perfect cup you have ever had.

The coffees of Yemen and Ethiopia, the only two countries where coffee is a native plant, faded in popularity for a while. Yemen's self-exclusion from world coffee trade organizations during the 1980s also hurt the marketability of its homegrown beans. Now that Yemen is back in the fold, so to speak, it is gaining a wider audience. The Harar of Ethiopia varies greatly, but when it's great it's spectacular, and the sweetness and smoothness of classic Yemen Mocha, one of the few dry-bean coffees to make most coffee vendors' Top Three list, is as wonderful today as it has always been.

What about flavorings? Spices have been added to coffee since the first adventurous brewers crushed the beans and put them into water. For centuries, cardamom, cinnamon, cloves, even pepper, have found their way into coffee. Nowadays you'll find such additions as fruit-flavored syrups, orange peel, cinnamon sticks as stirrers, and everything else imaginable. Some blenders, even some who sell flavored coffees, think it's a crime, an abomination except as a "cultural" experience. Others are only slightly less caustic, saying only that flavorings "bruise the brew."

When you drink a flavored coffee, you're tasting the flavoring over and above the coffee. My advice? Try finer selections of coffee over your store-bought canned, preground varieties. If you still don't like the flavor of specialty arabica bean coffee, brewed properly and simply, either go for flavorings or try another beverage. It's your dime.

As for decaffeinated coffee, it always makes me think of the orange spout on coffee shop carafes that shout to the world, "I am decaf, I mean no harm."

Decaffeinated coffee was actually discovered by accident rather than intention. Ludwig Roselius, a coffee importer from Germany, received a shipful of coffee beans one morning in 1903, in itself an unremarkable event. Roselius soon discovered, however, that the beans had been soaked to a fare-thee-well by seawater as a result of a tremendous storm that had engulfed the ship. Not one to throw out the beans with the seawater, Roselius decided to have the beans tested to find out whether or not they could be saved (and sold, of course). The lab reported that most of the caffeine had been stripped away. Recognizing opportunity out of disaster, Roselius invented a technique to strip coffee of its caffeine, using clean water, and he named his new coffee Sanka (from the French *sans caffeine*, "without caffeine"). That's why, when you stop by an American coffee shop or small restaurant, the waitress can come to you with one brown- and one orange-spouted carafe.

A few decaffeinated blends made with water filter processes are smooth and mild, but at best they are just okay. I admit that, on the whole, I abhor decaffeinated coffees because they lack the "kick" I love about coffee. If you really, truly don't like or are allergic to caffeine, even in the smaller amounts found in an espresso cup, skip coffee and go for juices and waters rather than the decaffeinated stuff; at least real juice is real food.

My feeling about decaffeinated coffee is best summed up with an actual incident I had at a lovely Italian restaurant where several friends and I had just had a scrumptious meal. We were ordering coffee to cap it off. One friend said, "I'll have a decaf espresso, please."

The waiter looked up from writing our order and asked, "Why?"

Why indeed. A little bit of caffeine is not only acceptable, it's good for what ails you. The problem with many Americans and their use of caffeine (like everything else) is that they drink twenty cups of mediocre coffee a day instead of a modest amount like two or three cups of high-quality brew.

It's hard to beat the convenience of a can of coffee and an automatic coffeemaker. My argument for freshly ground beans and a maker suitable to the bean and its grind is that what you'll end up with is pure pleasure. You will, most probably, drink less, but drink better coffee and get much more out of each cup. It is always worth it to give yourself this gift of fine coffee. While some critics insist that studied connoisseurship is precious behavior, making the simple an art form is good for the soul. I salute all those who think that preparing coffee well is a satisfying part of everyday living.

In this book, we will dip into the treasure trove of poems, music, and revealing quotes that coffee has inspired, offer a few contemporary coffee moments, commentaries from world-class coffee drinkers of today, and offer you some coffee trivia, facts, and lore. We will show you how coffee is enjoyed in other than the typical coffee-drinking countries and demonstrate that wherever coffee is enjoyed, you will find some form of the coffeehouse, whether it be a humble meeting place in a village or an ornately bejeweled icon in a city, literary salon or hotbed for political revolution, or simply a comfortable place to talk, read, hear music or poetry, play board games, or just be.

Auntie Mame, one of my favorites of Patrick Dennis's many memorable characters, said it best: "Life is a banquet, and most poor suckers are starving to death." They're starving because they scarf down quantity over quality, use convenience over artfulness, and neglect to perform the everyday rituals that make living a constant pleasure.

There are few pleasures that are so easy to find, so inexpensive to buy, and so simple to prepare as a great cup of coffee—why shouldn't you seek out affordable luxury every day? Make fine coffee your everyday passion, and you'll be feasting at the banquet of life.

Enjoy!

—Diana Rosen

The postman always drinks twice

THE
Coffee Lover's
COMPANION

"Oh, fortunate are those whose hearts have often been warmed by this sweet drink!" GUILLAUME MASSIEU

WHITE HOUSE
GROUND
COFFEE
DWINELL-WRIGHT COMPANY
ONE POUND NET

PERHAPS you have tried many brands of coffee. Changed pot or percolator time after time. Followed directions faithfully. Yet you have not been able to make your coffee unfailingly good.

Try White House Coffee. All the good coffee taste has been *roasted in.* All the natural fragrance retained. The coffee you make will come to your table, golden brown, delicious. Your husband will leave home happy in the morning. Your guests will linger over the dinner table at night.

© 1926, D. W. CO.

The Flavor is Roasted In!

DWINELL-WRIGHT COMPANY

Boston   Chicago   Portsmouth, Va.

LEGENDS AND LORE

A COLLECTION OF COFFEE FABLES

❖❖❖

Every woman believes she knows the secret to a man's heart. For some, that secret is a divinely prepared meal; for others, it's art and skill in the boudoir; for Helen Rowland, writing in the old *New York Evening World*, it was decidedly coffee. Here is the first verse of her poem, *What Every Wife Knows*.

Give me a man who drinks good, hot, dark,
strong coffee for breakfast!
A man who smokes a good, dark, fat cigar
after dinner!
You may marry your milk-faddist, or your
anti-coffee crank, as you will!
But I know the magic of the coffee pot!
Let me make my Husband's coffee—and
I care not who makes eyes at him!

1

Give me two matches a day—
One to start the coffee with, at breakfast,
and one for his cigar, after dinner!
And I defy all the houris in Christendom to
light a new flame in his heart.

Where did this "magic of the coffee pot" come from? How did our ancestors learn to take a shiny red cherry, roast it, grind it, add water, and drink the brew? The answer is the same for most foods and beverages. They came to be served in their acceptable way by trial and error, plus a dose of imagination. The adventurer experiments, trying the new food raw, adding it to foods already known, or, as in the legend of Khaldi, observing how animals approach a new food. Thank goodness for those who pursued their fascination enough to take a raw, bitter fruit and experiment with it enough ways to learn how to turn it into a hearty beverage with a deep, delicious taste.

Although the legends and myths about the origins of coffee still charm, they never seem to be as valid as a scientific report or medical analysis can be. The earliest written remarks about coffee are attributed to an Arabian physician, Rhazes, who lived in the tenth century. His book leads to the largely accepted viewpoint that Ethiopia is the birthplace of *Coffea arabica*, which still grows wild there. The native plant grew in the high plateau, along Lake Tana, and has, at one time or the other since then, been found in Angola, the Congo Basin of Zaire, the Cameroons, French Guinea, Sierra Leone, Liberia, and on the Côte d'Ivoire (Ivory Coast).

Coffee was first cultivated at the southern tip of the Arabian peninsula, in Yemen, in about A.D. 575 which gives credibility to the idea that Arabian traders brought coffee, and Ethiopian slaves, to Yemen. They were not the only ones transporting coffee, as the Persians carried coffee with them when they overthrew Abyssinian rule in Yemen in A.D. 570. As dramatic as that was, it had virtually no impact on the growth of coffee as a worldwide beverage, as its use was unknown outside of Arabia until the fifteenth and sixteenth centuries—a fact some historians attribute to the Arabs' attempt to control the commerce of coffee. They blocked all transport of green coffee beans (which could germinate), and held their prized place in the marketplace for years.

Some historians believe that the seven expeditions to the Red Sea and the African coast led by Cheng Ho, a Chinese admiral, in the early 1400s, brought the concept of an infused hot beverage to the Middle East, and the idea quickly caught on, fostering the first public coffeehouses in Mecca and Medina about 1470.

Admiral Ho brought with him his own drink of hospitality, brick-tea, molded slabs of compressed tea leaves which were grated and boiled, much like the "Turkish" style of coffee later developed by the Arabs. Although the Arab traders had known of tea since the ninth century, it was unusual to view someone drinking tea for pleasure rather than as a medicinal tonic. The adoption by the Arabs of the use of small china (porcelain) cups, further gives credence to the influence of Chinese traders in the Arab world. Rather than the small cups, Persians (Iranians) and northern Muslims used large dishes for drinking tea, the Turks did the same into the sixteenth century, and even in today's Yemen, very large, wide-mouthed cups are used.

THE HISTORY OF COFFEE

What makes the history of coffee so interesting is its legends; many are perhaps apocryphal, but that should not deter us from being enchanted by the possibility that they are based on fact. What we can rely upon as truth (truth being a collective agreement on what is true) is that the coffee bean originated in present-day Yemen and Ethiopia, was carried about by native nomads and by traders, both foreign and domestic, and eventually traveled full-circle around the globe. It was pursued avidly by enthusiasts of the beverage made from this red, cherrylike bean, and, as with all things popular, for the commerce it could foster.

Today coffee is a vital category on the vigorous commodity markets of the world, yet its historic battles and drama continue: Omnipresent clouds of inclement weather, encroaching bandits, and fluctuating currencies influence its market value daily. Although the dominance of the main players in the coffee trade has shifted from Middle Easterners to Indonesians and Central Americans, coffee remains a beverage steeped in the tradition of hospitality, and it continues to cement business and personal relationships in nearly every country in the world. Here follow legends about that glorious brew.

Muhammad and the Power of Coffee

One day Muhammad fell asleep, unable to keep alert to his duties. To his aid came the archangel Gabriel, who brought down with him from heaven a special concoction, a beverage we now know as coffee. He gently awoke the great leader and offered the reluctant hero a few sips. Muhammad was so quickly and thoroughly invigorated that he was able to "unhorse forty men and make forty women happy."

How long a period this took has not been recorded anywhere.

Legend of the Goatherder Khaldi

About A.D. 850, a herdsman in Upper Egypt (or the upland plains of Ethiopia or Abyssinia, no one knows for sure) noticed his goats became unusually lively after feeding on berries that grew nearby. The animals abandoned themselves to the most extravagant prancing, yet were still controllable and could be herded along. Eyeing the source of their pleasure, the brave Khaldi tried the beans himself and found himself feeling more alive and energized than ever before and more able to tend to his flock without fatigue during the long nights.

The abbot of a nearby monastery soon became aware of Khaldi's change of behavior and was fascinated with Khaldi's energy and alertness despite the strenuous demands of his goatherding duties. As skeptics did through the ages, the abbot at first thought these berries were the work of the Devil, so he threw them away, into a nearby campfire. Astonishingly, this action of distrust proved to be the key to turning the abbot on to the charms of the berry, for the fire naturally released the intoxicating aroma found within them. Lured by the exciting aroma, the abbot quickly plucked the berries from the fire and started to view them not as the work of Satan, but as a potential new food. He experimented with recipes and finally came up with the idea of mixing the berries with water, boiling them, and drinking the liquor.

This new beverage turned out to have remarkably stimulating results, and the abbot encouraged his followers to drink up. Of course, he also had an ulterior motive: This drink, like no other, could keep his followers alert while they recited lengthy devotional prayers, surely an apt strategy to protect a monastery against the evil of any devil.

LEGEND OF SHEIK OMAR

This legend involves another religious man, a Yemeni dervish, sometimes referred to as Sheik Hadji Omar, who somehow managed to be exiled from Mocha in 1258 on some unspecified moral failing, although it most probably was some offense against the government rather than any "sin," as some stories allege. Facing starvation and finding nothing but berries around him, he fell upon these, boiled them in a saucepan (we assume he was banished fully set up for housekeeping), and drank the thick brew.

Both a physician and a priest, Omar was quite a sophisticated man, so he naturally served his new brew to patients he treated while in exile. The patients, invigorated by this new medicine, sang his praises, which were soon heard back in his old hometown of Mocha. With all the good press he was getting, Omar was finally forgiven by the governor of Mocha of those unspecified "moral failings" and invited to return to his homeland as a hero, no less. The governor even built Omar his own monastery, where he was finally left in peace to sing praises to Allah while fully alert after drinking his beloved boiled berries.

LEGEND OF BABA BUDAN (OR THE BELLY BEAN STORY)

While visiting the Middle East in about 1600, Baba Budan patronized the coffeehouses and became enchanted with their beautiful furnishings and intrigued by their interesting patrons, who sat comfortably atop soft plush rugs, relaxing over their coffee while they talked. Poets, pundits, and coffee lovers alike were seen sipping upwards

of twenty cups a day while discussing serious issues, and the coffeehouse became the place for the ever-growing hordes of pilgrims visiting Mecca. (Granted the cups were small, even smaller than demitasse, but twenty cups of strong coffee was and still is a lot!)

Ever alert to opportunity, Baba Budan quickly realized what many other pilgrims did, that in addition to Allah, coffee was on the minds of everyone, Muslim or not. Seizing the moment, Baba Budan took seven precious coffee seeds, bound them to his belly underneath his clothes, and surreptitiously escaped the area with his theft unnoticed.

After arduous travel through mountains and deserts over many weeks, he finally reached his hometown in the hills near Chicamalagur in southern India. There, Baba Budan revealed to his neighbors his precious seven seeds. Planting them carefully, he nurtured them and lived long enough to see them flourish and grow and provide many hundreds of pounds of coffee beans to his community. Many coffee plants cultivated today by the people of Coorg and Mysore (Karnataka) may indeed be descendants of these seven seeds, but more likely, the Indian coffee industry owes its life to the British colonials who organized a plantation system and set up the necessary processing and export facilities in the 1800s.

Coffee has two virtues: It is wet and it is warm.
—Old Dutch saying

Saga of the Noble Tree

While the Venetians were instrumental in bringing coffee to Europe as an item of trade, it was the Dutch who literally brought the coffee plant to the rest of the world. The early Dutch explorers, fascinated with this new drink from Mocha, brought the first coffee plant from Mocha in Yemen to Holland in 1616. Then, after several decades of devotion to the drink, the Dutch realized they could grow their own in colonies that they then controlled. The first serious coffee cultivation by the Dutch was in Ceylon (now Sri Lanka) in 1658. Ever anxious to explore and own, the Dutch took coffee with them to Malabar in India and finally to Java in 1697, where it still grows.

Whether through Dutch influence or not, Louis XIV of France became an ardent coffee drinker. The Dutch, who owed him a favor, procured a single coffee tree for him, allegedly from Mocha, carried it aboard a ship to Java, then finally across the seas back to Holland and overland to the king's chateau in Marly, arriving in 1714. This sorry little plant, weary from traveling almost around the world, was transferred with great pomp and ceremony the following day to Paris's famed Jardin des Plantes, the first greenhouse in Europe, constructed to house the noble five-foot tree. It grew and blossomed and became one of the most prolific parents in the history of plantdom. From this single tree came millions of arabica trees, including those now growing in Central and South America.

These first sprouts reached Martinique in the Caribbean in about 1720, thanks to the heroic work of Chevalier Gabriel Mathieu de Clieu. Although he has been accused down the ages of stealing the precious shoots, it is more probable that King Louis XV put him up to the "theft" to give the Dutch some competition. Nonetheless he is a hero, who bravely fought off the Dutch, and numerous spies attempting to steal his shoot for greed, vengeance, or worse. He nourished and tended the small plant day and night while sailing the rocky seas, often giving his own ration of water to feed this ancestor to Caribbean coffee history. His devotion proved successful, and de Clieu returned to the Caribbean with the still-healthy shoot in hand. From this single plant have flourished millions of coffee trees, including those under cultivation in Santo Domingo, Guadeloupe, Haiti, Mexico, and most of the Caribbean islands.

The French were not always so successful, as the following example proves. One Francisco de Melho Palheta, a (Brazilian) captain lieutenant of the Coast Guard, was sent to French Guyana by the emperor of Brazil sometime between 1727 and 1735 (historians disagree once again). His visit to the governor there was ostensibly to handle a boundary dispute between French Guyana and Dutch Guyana (now Surinam). Actually, he was on a mission to obtain coffee seeds. So charming was he that the wife of the governor of French Guyana fell under his amorous spell. Eager to please the suavely conniving Don Juan, the lady carefully and secretly buried several precious coffee seeds in a bouquet of flowers that she sent to her beloved Palheta. The foolish woman thought a gift of precious coffee seeds would bind her to him forever. Palheta had other motives in mind. Clasping the French-owned seedlings to his breast, the cad never once looked back as he galloped home to the Portuguese colony of Para in Brazil, where his subterfuge helped the South American country become the largest grower of coffee beans in the world.

What Pleasures a Coffee House daily bestows!
To read and hear how the World merrily goes;
To laugh, sing and prattle of This, That, and T'other;
And be flatter'd and ogl'd and kidd'd too, like Mother.
—First verse of the song "The Coffee
House," by James Miller, 1737

The "gold" of Brazil soon moved to Sumatra in Indonesia and Goa in India, much promoted by Dutchman John Hopman, one of many Dutch traders to sell, cultivate, and promote coffee outside its natural homes of Yemen and Ethiopia. The Arabs themselves also carried their coffee tradition outside their own borders on their various invasions into Spain, North Africa, Turkey, and the Balkans, all of them following the more traditional Arab way of brewing the bean to this day.

The English took coffee to their colonies, beginning with cultivation in Jamaica in 1730, and India in 1840. The Spanish took coffee from Java to the Philippines, and Santo Domingo transported seed to Cuba. Later in the century, coffee was growing in Guatemala, Puerto Rico, Costa Rica, Venezuela, and Mexico. Seeds originally grown in Rio as early as 1825 were planted successfully in Hawaii and continue to flourish, the only truly "American" coffee.

Kona, which grows on the slopes of the Mauna Loa and Hualalai volcanoes, is the direct descendant of a coffee tree that first arrived in these islands in 1827 as a gift from England to Kamehameha II. Unfamiliar with this plant, the Hawaiians believed it to be purely ornamental. In time, it was replanted, and thrived in the volcanic soil. Kona has had its downs and ups, and it has only been in the last two decades that new coffee planting has been encouraged. Nonetheless, it still yields barely more than 20,000 bags per year.

Shoots of the "noble tree" continued on their worldly travels. At one time they were sent to the island of Reunion in the Indian Ocean, then known as the Isle of Bourbon. A different variety, with smaller beans, it was named Java Bourbon, and the famed Santos coffees of Brazil and Oaxaca coffees of Mexico are said to be the offspring of the Bourbon tree. The Santos coffee beans were named for Alberto Santos-Dumont, who became known as the coffee king, because he managed during his lifetime to oversee the planting of five million coffee plants in Brazil.

The beans could well have earned frequent flyer miles—although their mode of transport was by ship. They traveled a tremendously circuitous route from Ethiopia to Mocha to Java to a hothouse in Holland to a greenhouse in Paris then back to Reunion and then halfway around the world to Brazil and Mexico. Finally, in 1893, Brazilian coffee seed was introduced to Kenya and Tanganyika, only a few hundred miles south of its original home in Ethiopia, thus finishing a six-century circumnavigation of the globe. (The debate still rages on whether it was Yemen or Ethiopia that was the homeland of the coffee bean, but both places are the only ones where the plant is native to the area; for simplification, we are sticking with Ethiopia—don't write in protest, please).

The French took coffee to Tonkin (Indochina) in 1887, and even Australia got into the act when coffee was first successfully grown in Queensland in 1896.

Although coffee production is on the increase in both Hawaii and in some countries in Africa, the only "new" place for coffee growing in the last several decades is Vietnam, which has recently begun seriously growing robusta beans for export. The future, according to many involved in this new Vietnamese industry, is very positive. The country is now producing more than 65,000 tons a year.

COFFEE AND MEDICINE

In the early days of its use, coffee was most frequently thought of as a form of medicine. It was readily accepted as a stimulant and as a cure for digestive problems. Most certainly it was used to keep the devoted of various Muslim sects alert during their hours-long prayers.

Prior to the introduction of coffee as a stimulant, it had been a social custom in Aden to chew the fresh leaves of *qat*, which have a mild narcotic effect. This may have been the basis for first chewing coffee beans rather than using the subsequent method of making a beverage out of the boiled beans. The coffee bean (*bunnu* in Arabic) is surrounded by the *qishr*, a fleshy outer covering. It is sweet, containing a form of sugar and, at most, about 1 percent caffeine. Raw coffee beans were chewed for centuries in both Yemen and Ethiopia as well as many other parts of Africa and were valued for the slight buzz and energy-giving essence imparted by the caffeine. Much later, both *qat* and coffee were infused for beverages.

Before 1400 the Arab word *qahwa* referred to either wine or coffee, but sometime during the 1400s a beverage was made from the sweet *qishr*, or flesh of the bean. From then on the word for this became *qahwa* or some similar spelling or pronunciation of this word, which we know in English as "coffee."

Sufis and other Muslim sects used coffee for devotional purposes, to help them stay alert during long hours of prayers and to achieve a sense of enlightenment. The Sufis, who are a mystical faction that is a part of the Muslim umbrella of sects, considered the Islamic views of the relationship of man and God (as reflected in the omniscient, omnipotent, distant, and abstract straight-line Muslim theology of the fourteenth and fifteenth centuries) to be missing something, and, wanting a closer relationship with God, sought an emotional thread. They found what they were looking for in a variety of rituals.

The Sufis had many offshoots of their sect, each with their own rituals, many of which were intended to put the participant into a trancelike state in which they could achieve closer contact with God, forgetting the material world around them. All these rituals took place at night, some at mosques and some at *dhikrs* (meetings) at the homes of Sufi leaders. The *dhikrs* were not just a religious service but an important ritual, a reminder of the nearness of God.

Because of the fervor and the length of these meetings, coffee was quickly embraced. It was used prior to meetings by some sects, or used as part of the ritual itself in others. One common ritual had Sufi leaders carefully pouring coffee into a *majur*, a special large clay pot, then slowly ladling out cups with a special small dipper in a ritualized manner, from right to left, until the devoted were fortified enough to chant, "There is no god but God, the Master, the Clear Reality," into the night, along with their other devotions. The Yemeni Sufis, who traveled to Arabia and Egypt, took some of these coffee rituals with them wherever they went, but they were not seen in regular devotions in Syria, Turkey, or Egypt, nor do they appear in those countries much today, although coffee rituals are sometimes used by some Sufi sects in the West.

THE MAGIC BEAN

GROWING IT, PROCESSING IT, AND BREWING IT

✧✧✧

WHERE COFFEE GROWS

The world of coffee employs more than 25 million people, most of them in Third World countries, who grow, harvest, and process the beans prior to their being shipped to the United States and Europe. Many of these countries offer dry or unwashed coffee beans, which provide a full-mouth feel and a wilder flavor because they are dried out in the air in the sun and barely processed more. Washed beans go through many steps, with the end result being a bean that is as clean as it is pretty, and coffee vendors frequently take further steps to pick out deformities and broken beans so that what is left is "perfect."

Specialty coffee beans, on the whole, are arabica, washed and balanced for flavor and appearance. One can have an ugly, poor-tasting arabica and one can possibly have a nice-looking, good-tasting robusta, but the industry standard is definitely for

Arbre du Café dessiné en　Arabie sur le Naturel

washed arabicas of exceptional flavor. The work entailed to achieve this is considerable, which accounts for the price difference and definitely shows in the cup.

Because so many Third World countries, the source of most coffees, have declared independence from their colonial parents, names change. This can be confusing. For example, Zaire was once the Belgian Congo and rests just east of a country named Congo; they both produce coffee, but Zaire is a premier producer. The Mysore coffee of India is still regularly sold as such, even though it could be from Nilgiri or Coorg. Mysore is the name of a mountain and one of four divisions in the coffee capital of India, Karnataka. This is just a faint warning that if you see a coffee with an unusual name, it could be (1) a name change of an older coffee-growing country or province; (2) something "new," as Papua New Guinea is new, dating only from the 1950s; or (3) a misnomer, like Mocha, which is hardly ever what it once was, the premier bean of Yemen. Now it's a "type" of bean or blend. Those of you who like oxymorons, misnomers, or malapropisms can have a field day.

Your coffee retailer should be able to tell you what she is selling, where it came from, how it is processed, and what to expect in the cup. Unfortunately, some words in the coffee industry which have legitimate definitions have been stretched to their fullest marketing appeal. *Peaberry* denotes a small single bean (versus the large double flat bean), but the word is sometimes used to mean "exceptional bean," which it is not. To add more confusion, the word *caracol* is used for a region or country, when it is, in fact, Spanish for "peaberry," with the same meaning in Spanish as in English: the small, round, single bean of the coffee cherry.

As always, *caveat emptor;* make sure your coffee retailer is one who has educated herself. One benefit of shopping at the larger coffee chains is the superb attention to detail and conscientious seeking of fine beans that their buyers provide and the ensuing credible information pamphlets they provide. They have done their homework, and that makes it easier for you to learn about and enjoy better coffees.

The following are countries whose coffees are regularly available. Those which are less available are duly noted and are included here because they're beans worth seeking out.

Brazil

Although Brazil produces more than one-third of the world's coffees, it is primarily robusta and not arabica bean, earning them less "good press." Brazilian robusta is highly popular and quite an acceptable bean in Europe, because it creates a good foam on espresso drinks. Some people love the iodine taste associated with Rios, which is a popular bean for blends made with chicory.

Brazil also grows a botanical variety of *Coffea arabica*, the Bourbon, which first appeared on the Isle of Bourbon, now called Reunion. Bourbon Santos was originally obtained from the Yemeni Mocha seed, but today's Bourbon is a distinctly Brazilian plant because no trees or seeds have been brought in from the original source for more than a hundred years. Santos are small, curly beans that produce a rather smooth cup. Those from the hills of Mogiana, the coffee-growing region in Sao Paulo, reflect the original Bourbon strain of *Coffea arabica* brought to Brazil in the eighteenth century. Sao Paulo produces nearly one-third of all Brazilian coffees, and Brazil is the world's top producer overall.

The harsher "Brazils" are known by the names of Parana, Victoria, Bahia, and Rio and are frequently used in blends. The only "Brazil" to buy in the store is Bourbon Santos.

Burundi

This east-central African country produces about 34,000 tons each year of high-grade arabica beans that brew a cup with good body, high acidity, and rich taste. Good alone and excellent in a blend.

Cameroon

This republic in West Africa produces about 85,000 tons of coffee, but only a limited crop of arabicas, which are indeed sweet and mellow—a nice find for a change of taste. Their peaberry (small) and elephant (giant) arabica beans provide a sweet-drinking cup.

Colombia

The second largest grower in the world, Colombia produces its crops on the Andean slopes at an altitude of 4,200 to 6,000 feet and is the source of about 15 percent of the total world production (about 1,100,0000 tons). Supremo is the highest grade of Colombian coffee, with a rich, full flavor and mellow body; while not the world's finest, it is certainly a good-quality cup. Colombia Excelso is a top-grade Colombia with a more mellow flavor than Supremo, and a mild body. Medellin is a fancy, mountain-grown coffee of high quality with a dark green bean that provides a handsome roast and gives flavor and body in the cup.

Generally, Colombia is producing a bean that is more neutral, some even say bland, as the country itself opts for quantity over quality. Put the blame on Juan Valdez and his charming smile; although if I saw a coffee picker with a mule walking up and down the grocery aisle, I'd be highly suspicious of my grocer.

Costa Rica

Costa Rica is a cosmopolitan, sophisticated country with a high literacy rate and appreciation of music and the arts, and all of that is reflected in their beans; one can hardly get a bad one. Coffee is not a native plant to Costa Rica but was brought from Cuba in 1779 by the Spanish traveler Navarro. The most southern of five Central American republics, Costa Rica produces one of the finest coffees in the world, at a rate of nearly 170,000 tons per year. Coffee is grown in the Central Plateau near San Jose, the capital of Costa Rica, on small farms, 85 percent of which are now owned by Costa Rican farmers, rather than corporations or the government. The beans of Costa Rica are sharp in acidity and have a heavy body. Tarrazu is full bodied, robust, and rich, and considered by many connoisseurs to be one of the world's best. Some other names to look for are Tres Rios and Dota (both part of the Tarrazu region). Costa Rican coffees are all very balanced between acidity and body. They are good stand-alone coffees, reliable and delicious, but also wonderful additions to weaker beans for a complete blend.

Côte d'Ivoire (Ivory Coast)

Robustas are the beans here, and France gets most of them, although some U.S. instant coffee blenders have used them. A very distant cousin of the more famous and better African beans, it is grown on smallholdings in southern and central parts of the country. Coffee yield per year tops 250,000 tons, the greatest of any African country.

Dominican Republic

This West Indian republic on the Hispaniola Island produces Santo Domingo coffee, a blue-green bean that roasts up handsomely into a rich, fairly acidy flavor in the cup. The Ocoa, a washed coffee from this island, is one of the three best that are offered (the others being Cibao and Bani). These beans provide a comfortable acidity, pleasant taste, and good body.

Ecuador

Mild is the way to describe Ecuador's arabica-type coffee; it's not particularly anything, but this South American softens sharper beans in a blend. The country produces nearly 100,000 tons each year, no small crop.

El Salvador

With its mild, sweet flavor, the high-grown El Salvador bean is an excellent one for blending. The Central American country grows primarily coffee, in the west and northwest, at elevations of a modest 1,500 feet. Most of El Salvadoran coffee is good quality with medium to full body. The most exciting innovation in this country is the introduction of organic farming to its coffee farms in June of 1993. Since then, this farseeing country has produced the bulk of organic coffee, more than 150,000 tons of crop a year.

Ethiopia

Ethiopia produces primarily arabica coffee (some 225,000 tons) from wild trees in the provinces of Djimmah, Sidamo, Lekempti, and Salo in the west and southwest. Ethiopia is believed to be one of the two birthplaces of the coffee bean (the other, more established source, being Yemen). Addis Ababa, its capital, is the chief interior coffee market. The primary names for Ethiopian coffee beans are Abyssinian, Djimmah, and Harar, which is also known as Harrar and Harari. Harar is the most noted coffee of Ethiopia, grown on plantations near the ancient capital of Harrar, which is both a city and a province in the country. Coffee now known as Harar used to be sold as either Longberry Mocha or Abyssinian Longberry and is usually exported through Djibouti or Aden.

These coffees are described by connoisseurs as winey or fruity. The beans, except for those in Sidamo, are generally dry-processed. Yergacheffe is a more fragrant example of Sidamo and a wonderful stand-alone coffee.

Guadaloupe

This French American Dependency, an island in the Caribbean, is still hoping for independence from France and ships nearly all of its modest coffee crop to dear mama. It is excellent-quality coffee. Guess that means we must spend April in Paris, *oui*?

Guatemala

Some of the world's best coffees (close to Costa Rica, another world favorite), Guatemalans have overtones of chocolate or smoke, reflecting the volcanic topsoil in which they grow on the highland plantations. Guatemala still has strains from the orig-

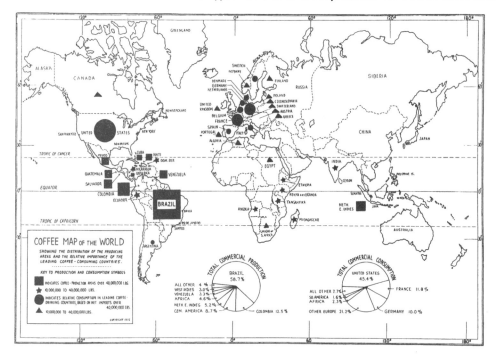

inal Bourbon tree and grows its crops in a greater variety of climates, all contributing to an interesting selection of beans. Some to look for are Guatemala Antigua, grown near Guatemala City, and Coban, a fruity bean. Guatemalans are sweet, with a full body and an almost spicy, smoky flavor that is rich to the palate. They are worth seeking out even if some snobs like to point out slight defects in appearance.

Haiti

Another West Indies island, Haiti offers a great blender bean, large, with a heavy body that produces a flavory coffee that some refer to as mild. Availability greatly depends on who's in charge today in the government; trade embargoes have decreased their tonnage produced to under 20,000. *C'est le café.*

Hawaii

The only coffee that is grown in the United States to any great degree, Kona is grown on volcanic soil, like Guatemalan Antiguas. It is a large, blue, flinty bean, mild in acidity and striking in flavor. Grown on the southwestern coast of the island of Hawaii, where the crop never faces frost, it has also been uniquely impervious to disease and insects, resulting in one of the highest-per-acre yield of any arabica coffees in the world. Still, it barely produces more than 20,000 pounds per year. An even smaller crop is being grown on Molokai and has been described as sweet, robust, and acidy. The Hamakua district also produces a good-quality bean. Kona is such a great lure for tourists that to get the best Kona, one really has to go to Hawaii. Reason enough to call your travel agent?

Honduras

This Central American country facing the Caribbean produces a fair-quality bean, that is small, round, and bluish green. A blender.

India

Karnataka grows 90 percent of India's more than 200,000 tons of coffee and produces the finest arabica bean from South India, where it has been grown since the seventeenth century. Its most famous growing division, Mysore, produces a bean that is similar to Sumatra beans in its deep color, low acidity, and full body; it makes a very satisfying cup, and at a lower price. When it's good, it's great; otherwise, it's still good. It is grown around the mountains of Mysore near where the first systematic plantation was established in 1840 by the British. (Yes, the same country that brought tea to India.) Mysore beans are sometimes misrepresented and may, in fact, come from

Coorg, Nilgiri, or Malabar, an area now known as Kerala. The Malabar bean, in particular, is different in taste from the Mysore bean and is a dry arabica very popular with those who like the mellow Indonesians; its small, blue-green bean yields deep color in the cup and a strong flavor. Another good grade of Indian coffee is the Tellicherry, but it's not always readily available.

Indonesia

First produced in 1699 by the Dutch government using forced native labor and plants from the Malabar coast of India, Sumatra coffees have become among the world's finest. Grown on one of the 13,000 islands of this archipelago nation also known as the Malay Archipelago, Sumatra coffees are distinguished by their deep-toned acidity and full body and are quite wonderful with milk. Grown near the port of Padang in west central Sumatra, an island in Indonesia, it is a medium- to high-grown coffee (2,500 to 5,000 feet). Sumatra is an extraordinary bean and is actually half-washed, half-dried, and known by two primary names: Mandheling and Lintong. A third Sumatran, one that is fully washed, is Gayo Mountain, but it has hints of spices, something you either like or not.

Indonesia produces some of the richest coffees in the world, 425,000 tons of it, making it the third largest producer, after Brazil and Colombia. They are, admittedly, some of my personal favorites, wonderful alone, with a full body accented by the dry processing. They add a richness to any blend. Among the popular coffees from Indonesia are Celebes (also known as Sulwesi), richly flavored with a heavy body. It is grown on the island of Celebes in the middle of the archipelago, as is Kalossi, grown on the nearby island of Toraja.

The Java coffees of great repute have decreased in taste and style; the plantations do not have the arabica trees they once had. Maybe in the next lifetime.

Jamaica

Yielding a highly acidic cup, and a fair taste, Jamaica Blue Mountain or High Mountain Supreme are debatable coffees; I suspect most people lust for them because they are so exclusive and rare. Compared to the Indonesians, even the famed Wallensford Estate Jamaicans pale considerably—another example of famous in the world but not great in the cup. As for quality, it is not even close to some of the glories from Costa Rica or Guatemala, although the Japanese, Jamaica's chief customers, obviously think otherwise, spending upwards of $15 million per year on this most famous bean.

Kenya

One of the world's best, this is another example of a "winey" bean, with a full-bodied, acidic taste that has a distinct tang. Although coffee is indigenous to the African continent, coffee in Kenya came from the Isle of Bourbon (Reunion) with the Roman Catholic missionaries as late as 1893. Kenya is considered the Switzerland of East Africa for its fine quality and tremendous export of nearly $1^{1}/_{2}$ to 2 million bags a year (about 225,000 tons) of beans grown on about 300,000 plantations. Grown at high elevations (5,000 feet), these carefully washed arabicas are consistently great; the ones with a blackberry overtone are even greater. The designations of AA and AAA and, sometimes, AA+ are more marketing than cup quality, but basically indicate larger size. I think they make a good espresso and certainly an exceptional stand-alone cup. Ironically, Kenyans drink their other famous crop, tea, and sell all of their coffee crop.

Mexico

The finest Mexican coffee is the delicate, fragrant, and sweet Pluma Altura, which grows in the south of Mexico. Other varieties to seek are Coatepec and Jalapa, for great aroma and sharpness—a good blender. When buying Mexican coffees, ask for those designated primo lavado ("prime washed") for exceptionally fine beans in appearance and flavor.

New Guinea

The Plantation A grade from Papua New Guinea is a rich coffee with a medium body and a slightly winey flavor. Although only produced since the 1950s, it has become a premier coffee of this small independent state northeast of Australia. Often lumped with Indonesians, it is in a class of its own—a washed, pretty bean with a good cup. Its acidity and nutty sweetness make it a nice addition to espresso. Often referred to as New Guinea or by its proper island name, Papua New Guinea, these beans are part of an annual crop of nearly 50,000 tons.

Nicaragua

The largest of all coffee beans, the Nicaragua Maragogipe yields a full-bodied cup; its sister Matagalpa, on the other hand, is boldly acidic with a very distinctive aroma.

Peru

Peruvian beans make a thin-bodied but flavorful cup. They have been steadily working their way into the top group of coffee beans. While not in the top ten, they are fine arabicas and worth trying, particularly those from the high Andes Mountain areas of San Martin, Cajamarca, Piura, and Lambayeque. Coffee beans from the Peruvian Chanchamayo Valley are considered some of the country's best, mildly acidic, thin-bodied but flavorful, and similar to lesser Mexican coffees. Peru produces about 85,000 tons of coffee a year, a quite respectable amount.

Puerto Rico

This island produces a bean that is excellent for dark roasting and a perfect accompaniment to the delights of Puerto Rican cuisine. These are beans of superior grades, ranking among the best in the world, producing a cup with a flavor similar to a washed Caracas Venezuelan, but much smoother. Technically, we could call this an American-grown coffee, because Puerto Rico has, since 1988, been a U.S. dependency, but because it is not represented in Congress, that's that. The island's coffee is also not produced in great quantities, so it is rarely exported, even across the bay to Florida. Another reason to call the travel agent?

Tanzania

The Tanzania is most often a peaberry bean, smaller and rounder than most coffee beans, which are double beans to each cherry and flat. This one is sharp with a winey acidity yet very rich in flavor. Similar to Kenyan coffee but thinner, arabica coffee from this East African country is sometimes still referred to by its former country name, Tanganyika. The finest is the Kibo Chagga, cultivated by the Chagga tribe in the upper slopes of Mount Kilimanjaro. Moshi or Arusha, named for shipping ports, are other Tanzania coffees. A robusta, Bukoba, is low bean on the totem pole, but Mbeya, an arabica, is an interesting blender.

A. GRIEVE

Venezuela

Not unlike its Colombian neighbors, the Venezuela bean is low in acidity, sweet, and delicate with a slight aroma, making it a good blending coffee, particularly the Tachira, a western-grown bean with a woody flavor. The best Venezuelans grow in the basin of Lake Valencia, west of Caracas, inland from Puerto Cabello. Although Venezuela is quite close to the Colombian border, its beans do not produce Colombia's characteristically full-bodied taste. Look for Maracaibo, Venezuela's best, with a delicate winey taste, softly aromatic, which makes it good for blending; Merida, a delicately flavored coffee sometimes classified as Maracaibo and most worthy; Trujillo (an undistinguished bean); Tachira and Cucuta (rich acidity); or seek a Caracas Blue, well known but an otherwise modest bean.

As for the Venezuelan Tachira, here again the name's the thing. Tachira-Venezuela is sometimes known only as Tachira but was once sold as Cucuta. To make things more confusing, Cucuta is now sold as Cucuta-Colombia. Go figure.

Yemen

The Republic of Yemen (Al-Jumhurijah al-Yaminyah) lies along the Red Sea in a section of old Arabia and is the official birthplace of coffee, despite Ethiopia's argument. Yemen's finest beans are known as Mocha, Mattari, Sharki, and Samani. Most Yemen coffee beans, a yearly crop of about 8,000 tons, are still dried with fruit attached to beans and husks removed by millstone, which accounts for the rough, irregular look of the beans. Sharki is an exceptional coffee, considered second best after Mattari and better than Sanani, which is grown in the Sana region.

Mocha—perhaps Yemen's, and coffee's, most famous bean—is named for the Al-Mukha port on the Red Sea coast, which supplied all of the world's coffee trade until the end of the seventeenth century, when a sandbar closed the route. A misnomer to be sure, mocha is also a common name for a drink made up of coffee and hot chocolate in equal parts.

Mocha-Java is the name of the world's oldest blend, which originated with one part Arabian Mocha and two parts Java Arabica. One classic blend, impossible to replicate today, contained equal parts of pure South Yemen beans with Java estate for a full-bodied cup with chocolaty overtones. Because today's Java beans are not nearly the same quality anymore, this blend can only be implied with substitutes for many variations on this theme.

Still grown as it was in A.D. 600, on irrigated terraces clinging to the sides of semi-arid mountains, the beans of Yemen are small and irregular, olive green to pale yellow, but in the cup they show a unique winey character with a heavy body and extraordinarily smooth flavor. It is still grown, cultivated, and prepared by hand, with the beans dried in the sun on cracked, dried earth. (Many Yemenis prefer *qat* to coffee, and Kenyans drink tea; so much for "You are what you drink." *Qat* is a leaf from a shrub indigenous to Yemen which is chewed for its narcotic effect or brewed as an infusion.)

Yunnan (China)

Yunnan province offers a low-acid coffee bean that provides a rich and full-bodied flavor in the cup. Grown in southern Mainland China, near the Vietnam border, Yunnan is similar to the best Indonesian coffees, with the character of a Sumatran Mandheling and the low-acid sweetness of Karnataka's Mysore. It has the same spicy sweetness and hint of smoke found in Yunnan teas. Unfortunately, the Chinese are not as adept at brewing coffee as they are at brewing tea, so this is best drunk at home rather than on your next trip to Beijing.

Zaire

Our final geography challenge: the Republic of Zaire has been known by not one but two previous names: the Belgian Congo and the Democratic Republic of the Congo. Like the rose by any other name, Zaire coffee beans are high-grade unwashed arabicas with high acidity, rich flavor, and very good body. The two best coffees are from Kivu and Itur, and, because they grow so near the Rwanda-Burundi border, they are similar to those arabica beans; they make good blenders. Only about 10 percent of their very plentiful yearly crop of 98,000 or more tons per year is exported. Alas, Belgium (no hard feelings apparently), Italy, France, and Switzerland get the bulk of Zaire's beans.

GROWING, PROCESSING, AND BREWING

Growing the Beans

Coffee beans grow at relatively high, usually mountainous altitudes in tropical climates, primarily in the band extending 25 degrees north and south of the equator. High-grown mild coffees (*Coffea arabica*) are grown at altitudes of at least 2,000 feet above sea level; their usual altitude is between 4,000 and 6,000 feet.

The term *Brazilian* refers to lower-grade coffees grown at low altitudes and mass harvested, and not to coffee grown in Brazil (which only produces mild coffees), thus *Brazilian* in this sense is a misnomer. Commercial coffees have large proportions of Brazilian, as do most instant coffees.

Robusta coffees (*Coffea robusta*) are highly resistant to disease and grow well at lower altitudes, but do not have the fragrance or flavor of the best arabica coffees. About twenty countries, primarily in Africa and Southeast Asia, produce robustas, which account for about 25 percent of the world's coffee production. The remaining 75 percent is composed of arabica beans with a tiny bit of other varieties. Most robustas, particularly from Brazil, end up in Europe, where they are used for espresso and table blends with great regularity.

Some countries, such as Colombia and Costa Rica, do not produce robustas at all, so you can be sure that if your canned or specialty coffee is from either of those two countries, you will be getting at least a modestly good arabica bean. What the specialty coffee lover is seeking is that 5 percent of the crop that is very good arabica out of the 20 percent that is distinctly good. The remaining 80 percent of arabicas frequently have numerous defects that account for their being less desirable on many levels. Despite what the prevailing commentary is, most canned coffees sold in the United States are *not* robustas.

Aged coffee is an anomaly. As a general rule, you want to buy the freshest beans that have been roasted fresh for you, but here is a bean that has been intentionally aged for those with an acquired taste for this brew. Aged green unroasted coffee beans have reduced acidity and increased body. Such coffee is held in special warehouses for long periods, sometimes as long as six or seven years, longer than either old-crop or mature coffee. The cup has a syrupy, dull, sweet heaviness with a woody, funky smell and taste, and here again you either love it or hate it. Aged coffee is also known as vintage coffee.

Cleaning the Beans

The purest, clearest brew of coffee in your cup is the result of slaves to cleanliness all along the route from grower to you. Although Third World countries work hard to grow some of the world's best coffee, they do not always end up with the cleanest beans, by far. A quick

look at the bags of beans will find some scented with spices because they were packed too closely with other products delivered in the same ship; or bags of roughly stitched fabric that allow dirt, or worse, bugs, to seep in. And the bags are rarely uniform, often varying greatly in weight.

Coffee workers in these poverty-stricken countries spend some time picking but more time guarding their trees from malevolent bandits, hungry animals, and other foes of their precious income-producing crop. They pick the beans, dry them (or wash them as the case may be), sort them, pack them (oftentimes sloppily but nonetheless sincerely) in rough burlap bags, and ship them out to brokers. At the green-bean roaster, these green beans must be thoroughly sorted to eliminate things you may not ever want to know existed: bullets, spent and otherwise; coins; rocks and pebbles; broken beans; broken bones and, on occasion, a fingertip or two. (Don't ask.)

Most arabica beans are processed by a wet method and referred to as "washed" beans. Other beans are processed by a dry method, by air or by the sun.

In either process, the object is to take off the hard shell, remove the skins, and get to the berry. The coffee bean has three sets of skin and one layer of pulp that form around the bean. One skin is called the pulp, which covers a sweet-tasting gummy substance surrounding each of two flat-sided beans and a single rounded one. Each of these beans is wrapped in a tough outer parchment and a delicate inner silver skin. All of these natural protective coverings are removed before the "brown gold" leaves the coffee plantation.

Beans are selectively picked as they ripen. The outer skin is immediately scraped loose, exposing the pulp. The beans are then soaked and the sweet pulp is loosened off the bean. More soaking and more washing occurs, and then the bean is dried. The last layers of the skin, now dry and crumbly, are stripped off the bean, exposing what is now referred to as the green bean. Some are polished to improve appearance.

In the dry process, waste material like stones, earth, twigs, and withered cherries are removed, and a preliminary cleaning is done. The berries are then dried via machines or, in poorer countries, dried on the ground or on boards out of doors. The berries are dried to a moisture content of 13 percent. Next, the berries are shelled and hulled and the dry pulp and parchment skins further removed as required.

Then comes a grading process, either by hand or by machine, in which the beans are separated according to size, density, and color. At the same time, fragments or flawed beans and any by-products like slubs (bits of the husk) are removed. The graded beans are sacked and sent to green brokers, who will test-roast and cup, then off they go to wholesalers to be roasted, blended, and packaged before they come to you, the consumer.

The washed method provides fewer imperfections and higher overall quality beans. In the washed method—the preferred one for arabica specialty coffee beans—the first step is to clean the beans by placing them in a tank of water. The ripe fruit is passed through a pulper, which removes the outer skin. The gummy residue is removed by open-air or tank fermentation before the beans are washed again in basins or washing machines before drying. They are shelled and hulled and separated according to size by machine or by hand to complete the preparation process before they travel to your coffee merchant's shelves.

At every step of the way, the intent is to clean, clean, clean the beans so that residue from the parchment and flawed beans are eliminated, producing an unbroken, fully formed bean ready for the coffee artist, the roaster.

Roasting the Beans

Roasting is both a science and an art. Entire books have been devoted to this critical part of coffee making; what follows here is merely a synopsis.

With the sophisticated machinery now available, temperature gauges are more accurate, timers can be set, see-through glass windows give the roaster an ongoing view of the process, and even roasting waste matter can be neatly eliminated and recycled as fertilizer. That's the science of it all. The art is the sensitivity of the hands, the eyes, and even the ears of the roaster to his precious responsibility, the coffee bean.

Not all roasting machines are supervised by human beings and watched as carefully as they are in the smaller independent roasting companies. But those still managed by conscientious men and women show the skill brought to the bean, and may it ever be so.

Coffee roasting is hot, physical work, requiring concentration and dedication. The expert roaster learns how to coax the best part of the coffee from the roasting machine using a sixth sense about the many variables of time, air flow, internal temperature, and the heat source. He is keenly aware of any changes in sounds, sights, and smells, and how they can mean the difference between a perfectly timed and evenly-roasted bean and one loaded with such imperfections as slubs, burns, and other undesirables.

One of the arts a roaster can achieve is the careful combination of beans to make a signature blend. It is not enough to blend the mild with the acidic or the full-mouth taste with the richly aromatic. The expert roaster can do this and more because he or she understands how to blend components to complement each other for a well-rounded cup that is more than the sum of its parts.

Other factors in a roast are moisture and soluble solids. While roasters may name their roasts differently, an overdeveloped roast would be too dark and an underdeveloped one would be too light. Italian and French roasts are very dark and dark, respectively; Vienna, Full City, and City are various degrees of medium; and American, Cinnamon, and Scandinavian are light roasts. New York is a type of medium or City roast.

Pyrolysis sounds like a serious medical condition, but it is actually the chemical process which generates the distinctive aroma and flavor of coffee. Pyrolysis occurs at about 400 degrees Fahrenheit during the roasting process, breaking down the fats and carbohydrates of the raw bean into the delicate oils, and is the point at which the beans assume their remarkably darker color.

Grading the Beans

Basically, there are three criteria for bean quality: size (peaberry [tiny], small, large, or elephant [monstrously large]), appearance (it should be clean, shiny, and free of bumps, stones, chips, and ugly marks), and source (altitude and species). Although fine coffees are available from many sources, only a few have achieved greatness, and among these, some reputations are purely legends of memory rather than realities in the cup. In the end, like all food and beverage items, it is the elusive fourth criterion that counts: quality, or as the coffee industry calls it, cup quality—the taste and smell of the brewed bean.

Size and shape are important elements in a good roast. Small, hard beans are good roasters, but bigger beans are usually softer, so they require more careful roasting to prevent burning. Elephant beans, the largest of them all, need to be roasted more slowly, and the smallest, the peaberries, roast evenly and easily, and, because they are rounder, take an even roast better than the flat beans.

Color is an important factor in the unroasted bean. Even though unroasted beans are referred to as green, the colors range from a light sage to ochre to a blueish green or blueish gray or gray-green or even brown. Watch out for black beans, though, they are foul tasting, and red-colored beans indicate that some fermentation has occurred.

When roasted, beans are various shades of medium to dark brown; here again, if they're really black, they're probably too burnt, although to some people that edge is satisfying.

Ironically, sometimes the coffees that smell the most enticing and exotic have only mild flavor, while others that have vague aromas taste fabulous. The Spanish say it best, *Sobre los gustos no hay disputa*, "In the matter of taste there is no argument." Let your own palate guide you.

Grinders

There is no law that says one shouldn't buy coffee already ground. Professionally ground coffee will likely be uniform in the granule size most suitable for your brewing method of choice. A reputable coffee merchant should do the job reliably every time, although different employees grinding the same type of bean may certainly add slightly different nuances. In the long run, you need to carefully choose your grinder, be it a person or machine, the grind, and, of course, the bean.

Grinding coffee is a matter of freshness, and freshness always counts, particularly if you want to brew a perfect cup of coffee each and every time. As always, it's important to know your coffee merchant. Some careless merchants do not clean their grinders well. That means you could get a residue of someone's French roast in with your mild New York roast. Let your eyes be the judge as much as your other senses.

It's always better to buy smaller quantities of whole beans and grind to suit. My favorite grinder is a no-name propeller mill I bought on sale for $8.95 at the health food store. It has a cracked lid which requires my covering it with my thumb while grinding, and a temperamental push-button stop-and-start apparatus that nonetheless precisely grinds in fifteen seconds two tablespoons of coffee at a time, exactly right for one perfect cup. Uneven grinds can taint the taste of even the finest beans.

I save my elaborate multibutton burr mill for when I have company and want to grind more than two tablespoons at once. Even using this more sophisticated machine, I try to grind the beans only fifteen to thirty seconds, although I always seem to overgrind in both amount and style—proof positive that the more buttons on a machine, the more likely they are there for show rather than for function. The more exacting among us would like the most uniformly ground beans, but I've come to a truce in my own personal battle between woman and machine and simply pick out those overly large pieces to ensure that the result is an even grind. If a consistently uniform grind is of paramount importance to you, consider an investment in the Bunn Deluxe Grinder Model BCG; Bunn also makes a terrific at-home coffeemaker.

Different grinds require different times to brew; a ballpark guide is one to four minutes for fine grind, four to six minutes for drip grind, and six to eight minutes for coarse grind.

MILLSTONE

The millstone has been in continuous use for grinding coffee ever since clever coffee lovers learned to stop eating the berries raw, roast and grind them, and concoct a pleasurable beverage. Using a millstone to grind coffee is obviously a crude, time-consuming, and labor-intensive method, but it does work, and it is to this day used by many Yemenis.

Not to be tied around one's neck, for those who love old sayings. For the adventurous only.

MORTAR AND PESTLE

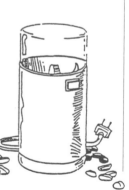

Also labor intensive, using a mortar and pestle is only slightly easier than using a millstone. But for those who have axes to grind or merely love to grind olive oil with fresh basil to make their own pesto by hand, this method is for you. I reserve a separate mortar and pestle for grinding only coffee beans because the volatile oils of the coffee beans will flavor anything they come in contact with. (Don't worry about this if you like coffee-flavored peppercorns or coffee-flavored pesto.)

ELECTRIC BLADE GRINDERS

These can be either push-button (propeller mill) or automatic (burr mill) and are fabulous for quick and easy grinding. Some models even have a series of multiple-choice buttons for determining the size of the grind. Like most food blenders on the market, no matter how many speeds or grind levels the machine may indicate on its buttons, I believe there is usually slow and fast, or fine and crude.

A blender, by the way, does work in a pinch, but takes a lot of stop-and-go checking along the way to get a truly even fine grind. I don't care if the manufacturer says it's okay to grind nuts or spices in their machines, they're wrong, wrong, wrong. First, the flavors will mingle, no matter how fastidious you are about cleaning the blender, and the oils in beans will coat foreign matter—making coffee-flavored cardamom seeds instead of the other way around.

Types of Grinds

Do you really need to measure coffee? How much should you use? Do various grinds call for different formulas?

Yes.

It varies.

And, yes.

Here's the deal: The coarser the grind, the more you need—because the coarser the grind, the more delicate the brew. Conversely, the finer the grind, the less you need, because the finer the grind, the more intensely flavored the coffee will be. (Hum it and you'll get it quickly.)

The various types of grinds are pulverized, very fine, fine, and medium, and each is used to make a different type of brew. Powdered or pulverized coffee, as finely ground as wheat is ground for flour, is used for Turkish coffee. Most grinders cannot grind fine enough, so seek out commercial grinders, unless you luck out and find an ancient Turkish grinder made especially for this style of brewing.

Very fine grinds should look like the texture of granulated sugar. They are used for drip or filtration coffeemakers such as espresso, *café filtre*, or Drip-O-Lator. Fine grind coffee should look like cornmeal and is just right for a Neapolitana, drip pot, or vacuum pot. Medium grind coffee is for coffeemakers that boil the coffee, such as a pumping percolator or electric percolator.

The main guideline is to be sure that the grinds are not too coarse or too fine for the holes in the filter basket or for use with paper or cloth filters.

Coffee should be measured by the scoop, and a scoop by any other name or apparatus is two measuring tablespoons—no less, no more. Forget the plastic scoops in the can. They usually measure out to one heaping tablespoon, not two level ones. And the scoops that come with various coffeemakers are no more reliable. Stick to a stainless steel or strong plastic tablespoon from a measuring set, and use your Pyrex measuring cup to measure out water.

All tablespoon measures in this book are for *level* tablespoons. For a typical dinnerware cup of six ounces of brewed coffee, use two level tablespoons of coffee plus six ounces of water.

For a twelve-ounce mug, use four level tablespoons of coffee plus twelve ounces of water. Adjust the recipe as needed, adding or reducing the amount of coffee to your taste. This is definitely a trial-and-error thing, but it is better to err on the strong side and cut the brew with hot water if needed. Coffee that is too weak has nowhere to go but down the drain. (If you are using one of the stronger Italian or French roasts, you should use slightly less coffee than indicated above.)

For four 6-ounce dinnerware cups of brewed coffee, use twenty-four ounces of water in your favorite brewer. Because you are brewing a pot rather than an individual cup, you will need less than the full two scoops of coffee per cup—I suggest six level tablespoons of ground coffee for the twenty-four ounces of water. Again, experiment to suit your own palate.

If you buy coffee already ground, use regular grind for percolators; drip grind for filter coffeemakers, drip pots, or drip makers; fine grind for vacuum makers or small drip makers; Turkish or finest powdered coffee for Turkish coffeemakers (*ibriks*) or, for a Turkish coffee substitute, use French or Italian dark roast beans ground into the finest possible powder coffee your machine can muster. Espresso coffee uses finely pulverized dark roast for *macchinetta*, or espresso makers.

> *Coffee is the common man's gold, and like gold, it brings to every man the feeling of luxury and nobility.*
>
> —Abd-al-Kadir, *In Praise of Coffee*, 1587

Sizes and Styles of Cups

How to drink your favorite dark brew? Shall it be in a mug, a cup, or a demitasse? What size cup for latte or espresso? It's really important to understand that a drip maker, for example, makes coffee geared for a six-ounce cup; now you know why you only get five mugsfull instead of the ten to twelve cups it says on the pot!

A. Grieve

Turkish coffee sets and Bedouin sets vary; some are small, demitasse size, from two to two and one-half ounces, while others are nearly five ounces or more. And if you're lucky enough to get a Yemeni saucer cup, that could hold nearly eight ounces.

Whatever receptacle you use, warm it up first before pouring in the coffee. Simply pour boiling or very hot water into the cup and cover with a saucer, then dump out the water prior to putting in your coffee. In this way your cup is heated, ready to receive the ancient "black broth" and keep it hot.

As for capacity, teacups and cups with traditional dinnerware settings usually hold six ounces; demitasse cups hold from two to two and one-half ounces. Mugs, on the other hand, vary considerably in capacity. Most mugs hold anywhere from eight to twelve ounces. To find out how much your coffee cup or mug really holds, fill a measuring cup with water and pour it into your cup or mug. Subtract the amount of water left in the measuring cup to determine your cup or mug's capacity. Now that you know the true capacity of your cup or mug, measure your coffee accordingly. You really only have to do this once, and you'll then be able to make an ideal cup or mug of coffee from now on.

If you want to use your lovely porcelain coffeepot, warm it first with hot water, then discard the water before pouring the prepared coffee into the pot. That way the pot will stay hot longer, the coffee will stay hot longer, and you'll provide your guests with coffee in the cup that's just the right temperature.

And what if someone wants a jigger of coffee? That's usually considered one and one-half ounces. You can put a jigger of coffee liqueur in your coffee or the other way around—just enjoy the thrill of the bean.

How to Brew a Perfect Cup

Chapter and verse have been written about how to brew a perfect cup of coffee, and it is amazing to interview coffee mavens around the country, both professional and amateur, and discover how many nuances there are and what tiny differences people adhere to in their methods of choice. Most coffee lovers shudder about boiled coffee, but over a campfire, after a long hike though the Smokies, nothing tastes finer. Other experts shake their head in feigned amusement that Mrs. Swensen from down the block refuses to give up her tall, striking percolator with its taped-up cord and polished stainless steel body even though her children swear by electric drip pots and her grandchildren have an Italian at-home espresso machine. If she's happy. . . .

Your own taste buds are always the final judge, but several things really do matter: freshness of the bean, freshness of the grind, and freshness of the water. In other words, every ingredient should be the best.

My personal choice is a Swiss gold filter that I set atop a years-old favorite terra-cotta-colored mug. I grind the New Guinea beans, throwing in a bit of dark-roasted Sumatra, and grind four tablespoons in my cracked, stained, push-button propeller mill. I heat up spring water in my electric kettle, and just when the bubbles become the size of those damn colored paper dots that spill out of invitations from people with a strange sense of fun, I pour the water in a circle, first around the outermost edge of the grounds in the filter basket, then farther inside, then I finish pouring directly in the middle of the apparatus. I lift up the filter to make sure the last of the pure coffee liquor has seeped into my mug, plop the filter basket into its elegant black matte bowl which I bought for that use only, and sit down and enjoy my brew straight, no sugar, no milk, no nothing. Ahh . . . now, that's real coffee.

This is not, of course, the only way I make or enjoy coffee, but it certainly is my favorite. I love the way the mug feels (the handle seems just right, not too heavy and not too flimsy), and I love the combination of my two favorite beans; both the aroma and taste seem to satisfy, without anything lacking.

The six elements to a proper cup of coffee are:

1. *Clean equipment:* Filters, coffeemakers, and other paraphernalia should be thoroughly cleaned after each use. If allowed to remain, the sediment can absorb odors, and the remaining coffee oils may turn rancid, tainting subsequent brews. A combination of baking soda and water is the best cleaning agent.

2. *Good water:* I prefer water that is slightly hard. It is a personal choice, of course, but I think artificially softened water tastes flat. Many people find that "neutral" taste quite acceptable, and softened water is certainly a good choice for espresso makers, which use finer grounds that may get clogged up in the filter basket if the water has too many other chemicals or organic wastes in it. Charcoal filters can screen out chlorine, chloroform, sediment, and organic waste, and they are a good choice for dedicated coffee drinkers. The TDS factor (total dissolved solids) recommended by most coffee experts is 150 to 200, so check with your city's water department; you may already be living in a good water source and not need any additional filtering of your water. If not, the Brita and other such filtering devices are fairly economical, easy to use, and last a long time.

3. *Proper temperature:* 200 degrees F, plus or minus 5 degrees, when water is in contact with the coffee grounds, and 185 to 190 degrees F when in the cup itself. Boiling water is not necessary to make good coffee.

4. *Proper grind:* The correct grind permits water to pass through the coffee in the correct time, leaving a minimum amount of sediment (Turkish and Arabian coffees excepted). The Bunn Deluxe Grinder Model BCG is a consistent machine that produces uniform sieve trails.

5. *Proper formula:* I cannot emphasize enough that personal taste is the end-all, be-all here. For individual use, consider as a starting point two measuring tablespoons (not flatware tablespoons) of coffee per six ounces of water. *Adjust for your taste.* For large-scale entertaining or commercial use, two to two and one-half gallons of water for each sixteen ounces of coffee; allow for a little leeway for evaporation of the water.

6. *Proper brewing time:* The optimal brewing time for all types of grinds is usually about four minutes. These formulas can be followed: One to four minutes for fine grind; four to eight minutes for drip grind; six to eight minutes for regular grind; 15 to 25 seconds is good for espresso with a pump.

Use a jug—it is not what you make in it, it is how you make it. It all hangs upon the word *fresh*—*freshly* roasted, *freshly* ground, water *freshly* boiled. And never touch it with metal. Pop it in an earthenware jug, pour in your boiling water straight upon it, stir it with a wooden spoon, set it on the hob ten minutes to settle; the grounds will go to the bottom, though you might not think, and you pour it out, fragrant, strong and clear. But the secret is fresh, fresh, fresh and don't stint your coffee.
—Florence L. Barclay, "Rosary"

Coffee brewers are not for just one person, for their capacity is so obviously suited for two or more people, and many are large enough for crowds. I do think that, as with any fine beverage, it's better to make coffee in small batches than in a big vat. Better to brew and store in thermal carafes than to brew a huge pot all at once. As for your choice of brewer, here are some choices with some wholly editorial viewpoints, mine alone. Experience is a great teacher, but the student has to bring his or her own sensibilities to class.

The Coffeepot as Brewer

Although coffee was used as medicine as early as A.D. 1000, that is no reason for your coffee to taste bitter or medicinal. The Arabs discovered that by putting boiling water on the coffee beans, a beverage could be made. It took them until the fourteenth century to discover how to roast the beans, but that's another story.

The choices among present-day coffee are not as wide as you might think. Most of them do pretty much the same thing: bring water and ground coffee together to produce a drinkable brew. As always, using the right ingredients and the right brewing system will produce a flavorful, rich, and delicious cup every time.

Extracting flavor from the bean can be done in two ways: *decoction* (boiling a substance until its flavor is taken out) and *infusion* (extracting flavor at a temperature below boiling via steeping). Infusion can also be achieved through *percolation* (dripping) and *filtration*.

In steeping, the simplest form of infusion, hot water is mixed with ground coffee. *Directions:* Heat to near boil fresh cold water in a pot, kettle, or pail. Remove from heat, add ground coffee, and stir. Cover pot for steeping for two to four minutes for fine grind, six to eight minutes for coarse. Just before serving, add a small amount of cold water to settle the grounds, then pour through a cloth or wire strainer into cups or a warmed serving pot.

In percolation, water drips through fine apertures in china or metal, but in filtration, water drips through cloth or paper. *Directions:* Heat water in a coffeepot or kettle, add coarse ground coffee, and brew for five minutes or more. Cold water can be added to settle the grounds (though many people use other clarifiers like eggshells and egg whites; even fish skin and salt pork rind have been used). Pour coffee through sieve or strainer into cups.

Glass and porcelain are the best materials; they retain heat easily, are simple to clean, and often are very attractive. Metal pots, especially silverplate and aluminum, can impart bitterness and astringency. Nonetheless, because they're attractive, and often so inexpensive, and easily available, coffee drinkers have for years used pots made from a variety of metals, from brass and copper in the Middle East, to stainless steel, nickel, aluminum, and plain or enameled tin in the West. If I had to choose one metal, it would be stainless steel, but I'm really partial to glass and porcelain for their ability to let the flavor of the coffee, and not the pot material, shine through. Let your taste buds be your guide.

The Bunn-O-Matic at-home machine is ugly, utilitarian, and without charm—but boy, does it make a good cup of coffee. The most important elements in this system are a dependable water reservoir and a heating element that heats the water within four minutes, the ideal suggested time span no matter what type of coffeemaker you use. You can find these makers at most appliance or discount stores, and they're certainly worth the investment.

Most coffee blenders I spoke to swore by either the Bunn-O-Matic, the vacuum pot or the French press pot, although one could make do with a pot on an open fire if left to one's own devices on a desert island. The benefits of the French press pot and the vacuum pot are that they are both self-contained, need no electricity, and can be either put on the flame or have hot water added to them, so they're clean, easy, and simple. Best of all, they each make a very smooth, clean cup of coffee. Here are some data on these and other favorites:

Coffeemaker Styles

(Unless otherwise noted, do not use any of these atop the stove.)

Timing is important: A pump percolator should take about six to eight minutes to brew; a drip or filter pot, four to six minutes; and a vacuum pot, one to four minutes.

FRENCH PRESS OR PLUNGE POT OR *CAFETIÈRE*

In this mechanical device, coarse-ground coffee steeps in freshly boiled water inside a glass cylinder. When the plunger mechanism is pressed down, the brew is separated from the grounds, producing a perfect marriage of French roast coffee and water. The grounds stay at the bottom of the pot, and all the coffee can be poured out at once into a warmed coffeepot. All-purpose or drip grind coffee is best, but a coarser grind is acceptable. Suggested steeping time is five minutes, but I prefer to stop at four. The longer you wait to plunge, the stronger the brew will be.

The more economically priced pots, from under $15, tend to be a little wobbly and the plunger a little less controllable, but they still make a delicious pot. Larger, fancier designer pots can climb past $225 and usually have a better metal filter screen and an easier-to-handle knob for pushing the screen down. To keep the end result hotter, first heat the pot with very hot water, then discard the water. Now you're ready to brew your coffee with a preheated pot. You can wrap up the pot with an absorbent terrycloth towel to further insulate it, or make your own "coffee cosy" by wrapping a quilted cotton placemat around the pot to keep in the heat.

CHEMEX

A handblown glass coffeemaker, with an elegant hourglass shape, the Chemex is as modern-looking today as it was when introduced in the 1930s by its inventor, Peter Schlumbohm. Although this coffeemaker makes a fabulous cup of coffee, you have to decide whether the upkeep is worth the taste. Because the pot is clear glass, every little stain shows, and it isn't easy to clean unless you have a teeny-tiny hand or a bottle brush cleaner that will bend like an S. For some people this is hardly an issue, because they believe the taste of the coffee brewed in a Chemex overrides any appearance issue. As a compromise, some friends of mine use it like a carafe for serving only, not brewing, then run it through the dishwasher twice to clean it thoroughly.

> *I set my timer for three minutes. Very methodical guy, Marlow. Nothing must interfere with his coffee technique. Not even a gun in the hand of a desperate character.*
>
> —Raymond Chandler, *The Long Goodbye*

VACUUM SIPHON OR VACUUM POT

This is comprised of a silver globe, a siphon, a strainer, and a mixing bowl. This double-barreled pot, which looks more like a rounded kerosene lamp than a coffee brewer, has gone through several modifications and still goes by several names. Those to look for are the Silex, that staple of the five-and-dime luncheon counter; the Cona, an elegant English model sometimes referred to as a glass balloon; the Bodum stovetop model; and a stainless steel version from Flavor-Seal, most sought after by those collectors who actually, incredible though it sounds, *want* those hideous yellow Formica and chrome tables and matching chairs with the stick-to-your-thighs seats.

Steam pressure is the method here, forcing the water to the top. Timing is important because you need to make sure the process is complete before removing the top globe and pouring from the bottom; four minutes minimum is the suggested time limit; one-half minute too soon, and you'll have globby coffee all over everything. A vacuum pot does make a fine cup of coffee with a medium grind of beans. Some models can be used atop the stove, and most can be taken anywhere without worry about proper electrical outlets. This device is a good American-style coffee machine for those who love a "brown coffee," a medium-fine nonoffensive grind, the one often called New York roast.

PUMP PERCOLATOR

Invented in 1825, this stovetop coffeemaker was quite popular during the nineteenth century, and many aluminum versions were evident in American homes during the thirties and forties. A percolator requires less coffee because the water is infused for a longer time. Simply pour the cold water in and boil atop the stove. Put medium ground coffee in the basket, insert the basket into the percolator, cover, and return to the heat. Allow to percolate for six to eight minutes. Remove the infusion basket of grounds and serve.

ELECTRIC PERCOLATOR

Whenever I think of the electric percolator, I think of the *bubble-bubble* sound it makes and the dance of the brew into the glass knob. It also reminds me of life in the Fifties in America, a quieter, gentler time yet one that enthusiastically if naively embraced the wonder of fully electrified appliances to make all our lives "easier." Whether they did or not is the subject for the tomes of sociologists, but certainly the automatic percolator freed more women, and men, to spend more time talking with one another and less time eyeing their coffeemaker.

The first percolator was invented in France by a jeweler, Jacques-Augustin Gandais, in 1827. His machine sprayed the coffee with water just once and resulted in an inadequate brew. Nicholas Felix Durant developed a percolator that raked boiling water over the grounds time and time again, resulting in a decoction. The automatic pump percolator, which some critics said further reduced the quality of coffee in the United States, performs pretty much the same but more quickly.

Most critics of the percolator eschew it because it boils the coffee rather than steeping it or infusing it in a gentler way. Technically, the water is heated, forced up through a center tube, and repeatedly circulated over the bed of coffee below, usually encased in a perforated metal filter. This, some say, results in overextraction. If you are enamored with New York City brews or just feel nostalgic for Elvis or *I Remember Mama*, then by all means drag out the elegant stainless steel icon of the forties and fifties and have a go at it.

MOKA

This very simple, very reliable stovetop non-electric espresso pot is all you really need to make espresso. It holds cold water in its bottom chamber and coffee in the middle basket, and the top container is used to help steam up the coffee water through the grounds and into the upper chamber. The moka makes an intensely flavored cup. Some come with a pump. Most Mokas are aluminum, which I think is dreadful, but stainless steel ones are becoming easier to find and usually cost under $30. Keep looking. As for fancier models, electric styles and the like, they're great for show and for flair but have no grounds for claiming a better cup, and that is, my dears, what it is always about. Some manufacturers refer to this style of coffeemaker as a mocha.

DRIP POT

Perfect for *café au lait*, this pot employs percolation (passing hot water though ground coffee and then through small holes into the pot below). Invented by the archbishop of Paris, Jean Baptiste de Belloy, in 1800, it was greatly favored by the food writer Jean-Anthelme Brillat-Savarin and was then called a *percolateur*, and had the traditional three parts: top for receiving water, bottom for receiving coffee, and a filter in between.

The *percolateur* was later refined by Count Rumford, an American named Benjamin Thompson, of Woburn, Massachusetts. About the black brew, he said, "Among the numerous luxuries of the table, unknown to our forefathers, coffee may be considered as one of the most valuable. It excites cheerfulness without intoxication; and the pleasing flow of spirits which it occasions . . . is never followed by sadness, languour or debility."

Count Rumford's drip pot had a device that kept the grounds compressed in their container, thus preventing them from agitation by the water. Today a drip pot still has the same three components: water receiver, coffee basket, and beverage receiver. Most popular is the aluminum Drip-O-Lator or a porcelain French *biggin*, a favorite among New Orleans residents. *Directions:* To use a drip pot, pour water that has just come to a boil through the water dispenser onto drip grind coffee in the removable section with a filter bottom. Preheat the serving pot and pour in the thick brew.

IBRIK

A long-handled tall copper or brass pot, the *ibrik* has no cover and tapers toward the top. Because Turkish coffee is boiled, it tends to be cloudy, even when clarified. When properly and fully boiled, the grounds in an *ibrik* do settle to the bottom. The brew contains a high concentration of caffeine. This type of pot is called a *briki* in Greece; it's politically correct to say Middle Eastern coffeemaker if you're not sure which you've got.

✧✧✧

A Coffee Moment

Miss D, Sausalito, California

I love a cup of very hot, very black Java right before I go to bed; it puts me right to sleep. Coffee has always relaxed me, and in some cases, it has almost saved my life. As an asthmatic, I drink coffee when I feel an attack coming on because it relaxes my lungs and air passages and helps me to breathe easier. Call me contrary, but coffee is my sedative of choice.

ELECTRIC DRIP MAKER

I love the convenience and ease of all these coffeepots; set 'em and forget 'em. I think many give the coffee a slightly bitter taste, particularly if kept on the burner too long. This may be from either using water that is too hot (typical temperature is best not boiling but between 195 and 205 degrees F) or surprising the innocent grounds with too much force instead of a gentle saturation.

These coffeemakers (Melitta, Krups, Mr. Coffee, etc.) are a simply conceived format, with hot water automatically heated and dripped through the coffee into a pot underneath that sits on a warming plate. The burnt taste that results when the pot has remained too long on the burner may actually be a result of chemical changes (polymerization of phenols or the naturally occurring chemical pyruvic acid, which is accentuated over a period of time). This burnt taste is not the same as that of overroasted coffee, a taste intentionally created in the roasting process.

Some models use paper filters (you now have a choice of bleached or natural papers), others use fine mesh filters, and that determines whether to use coarse or fine grinds, respectively. Since nine and one-half people out of every ten in all the world opt for convenience (especially if it comes with an alarm clock that will start the coffee for you), go for it. Some more recent innovations include a thermal carafe which permits the coffee to remain heated without burning or continuing to cook no matter how long it stays in the carafe. If the full flavor of the bean is at all important to you, however, choose another type of coffeemaker, preferably a nonelectric one at that.

NEAPOLITAN FILTER DRIP OR FLIP DRIP

Known in Italy as a *napoletana* or *macchinetta*, and used primarily for espresso, the Neapolitan is an upside-down pot because you put cold water in the bottom half of the pot, finely ground coffee in the filter basket and, when the water boils and its steam begins to escape from underneath the basket, you simply remove the pot from the stovetop, turn it over or "flip it," sending boiling water flowing through the coffee. The pot has two cylinders, one with a spout and one without, and a two-piece coffee basket that fits between them. The French counterpart, a *café filtre*, does a similar job without steam and pressure, and still provides a thick, rich brew.

It is no small act of daring to flip over the *macchinetta*, even with both hands and heat-resistant handles; there may be dribbles of water indicating that the entire unit is about to separate, sending burning coffee and waterlogged grounds over the counter or tabletop, and since most are made of aluminum, the coffee may have a metallic aftertaste. Nevertheless, here are the directions for using a *macchinetta*:

Pour cold water into the spoutless boiler and slip in the filter basket sleeve. Add coffee, three scoops or six level tablespoons, to one and one-half cups of water. Screw on the perforated lid and set the spouted container on top and the entire unit on the heat. When water is hot enough to spurt from the tiny holes at the top of the boiler, remove the entire outfit from the heat, invert the pot carefully, and allow the water to trickle through the coffee into the pouring section. Remove the boiler and filter sleeve, place the lid on the serving unit and pour.

Like espresso, coffee prepared in a Neapolitan filter drip should be served in demitasse cups or wineglasses; add a twist of lemon peel or sugar.

ESPRESSO AND CAPPUCCINO MAKERS

Home espresso machines are becoming more stylish and easier to use with each new model. They do not necessarily make a better espresso than a Moka, but that is my prejudice. Look for models with stainless steel filter baskets and sturdy glass carafes and make sure the tamper is made solidly.

The Easier Kind of Coffee
Made in the cup at the table

You make G.Washington's Coffee-by simply pouring on the water — It dissolves instantly — No coffee pot-No grounds-No waste — Simplicity itself and always a delicious cup of coffee. Quality always the same-Easily digestible-No harmful effects. Recipe Booklet free — Send 10¢ for Special Trial Size —

G.Washington's
COFFEE
Originated by Mr. Washington in 1909

G.WASHINGTON SALES CO.inc.
522 FIFTH AVENUE
— NEW YORK CITY —

Coffee Around the World

Customs, Anecdotes, and Some History of the Universal Drink

◇◇◇

Africa

"Dr. Livingstone, I presume?"
"Just in time for coffee, Stanley."

For centuries, coffee was a staple in African cultures which used coffee, not as a beverage, but as a solid food. The Africans would combine the beans with animal fat and chew them like nuts, enjoying their concentrated sweet taste. They often made thick flatcakes of pulverized coffee beans mixed with dried fruit and salted butter.

The African explorer, John Speke, wrote of discovering natives around Lake Victoria offering coffee in soup, but it is primarily as a "chew" that coffee is most likely to be found. The Somalis, for example, eat roasted and ground coffee solids mixed with toasted grains, and their craftsmen are famous for their specially created wooden mortars used for grinding up the coffee beans. The dried ripe skins of unprocessed coffee beans are sold as chews at native markets. Somalis and Ethiopians brew them into a beverage that tastes, some say, like straw.

Ugandans are particularly well known for their special woven baskets they make exclusively for these chews. Ugandans also mix green beans with sweet grasses and various spices, dry them, and then wrap them in grass packets to be hung in their homes as both decoration and talisman.

Among the many African countries that grow coffee are Zaire, Sierra Leone, Uganda, Ghana, Burundi, Nigeria, Rwanda, Angola, Congo, the Côte d'Ivoire, and, most importantly, Kenya. This "Switzerland" of Africa is the most notable coffee growing country on the continent, and one of the seven most important coffee countries in the world today. Because the land never experiences frost, the beans are highly acidic, heavily aromatic, and particularly sought after for blending with beans from other countries. Kenya has some 300,000 plantations and exports nearly all of its crop. The larger bean, named Kenya AA, is exceptional and added to espresso blends, provides a lovely aromatic kick.

Although coffee is not used as a beverage in most African countries, its marketability is well understood and it produces a substantial cash crop. As for their beverage of choice, most drink tea.

TURKEY

... little China Dishes, as hot as they can suffer it;
black as Soot, and tasting not much unlike it.
—A traveler, in the early sixteenth century,
writing about Turks drinking coffee

The first coffeehouses in Constantinople (Istanbul) opened in the mid 1500s and were much like the penny universities of London several centuries later. Called *qahveh khaneh*, "schools of wisdom," they were elaborately designed places where well-educated men of letters, scholars, and others would come together to discuss poetry, politics, and other cultural subjects. Musicians would play the songs of the day, and game boards were brought out to play chess or *mancalah* (from the Arab root word meaning "to move oneself or other things around").

Although some of the most famous drawings and artwork of Turkish coffeehouses reflects the use of the *nargileh*, a water pipe for smoking, the coffeehouse did not embrace smoking, certainly not until the late sixteenth century. One didn't go to the coffeehouse to get high on drugs, a practice then thought to be reprehensible; hashish, though rare, was then absolutely prohibited by law. Tobacco had yet to be introduced to the area, and it was not until the British traders brought back tobacco from the New World that smoking caught on to any degree.

What the patrons sought was the conviviality of the coffeehouse, and the coffee itself. All would listen to storytellers, some of them paid professionals although most storytellers entertained while still maintaining their "day job," a fact of life for artists in every generation. Storytellers sometimes accompanied themselves or had a musician with them who played the *saz*, a stringed instrument, which is very common even today, particularly in Turkey, where storytellers are still found at many coffeehouses. The old storytellers knew how to weave myth and truth into entrancing tales primarily about heroism—not unlike Homeric legends of the West. The audience for these storytellers were men, of course, because nice women didn't go to the coffeehouse, something they still do not do, except to "touristy" places in the main cities.

Although the women were excluded from coffeehouses, they did indeed drink coffee at home. At one time Turks who refused or neglected to furnish their wives with coffee created legitimate cause for divorce. Frenchman Fulbert de Monteith, upon hearing of this Turkish tradition, said, "Perhaps it is more prudent than to swear to fidelity."

Francis Bacon was quite enchanted with this type of coffee and said, "Turkish coffee was made of a Berry of the same name, as Black as Soot and a Strong Scent but not Aromatical; which they take, beaten into a Powder, in Water as Hot as they can Drink it, and they take it, and sit at it in their Coffee Houses, which are like our Taverns. The Drink comforteth the Brain and Heart and helpeth Digestion."

In nearby Iraq, during the 1600s, entertainment centered around the *Maqam*, or poems recited by a group of five *chalgis*, a singer and four musicians, where the guests would sit for hours on end listening to the oft-repeated melodies, sipping coffee, and later tea.

Jean-Baptiste Tavernier's book *The Six Voyages*, published in 1676, describes his travels to Turkey, Persia (Iran), and India. He writes of the mystery and charm of coffee, as did others of his fellow travelers from England who bravely ventured into the Levant and through the Middle East in those dark days of difficult travel in the sixteenth and seventeenth centuries. Here is what Tavernier had to say about Isfahan at the end of the seventeenth century:

Under the arcades are situated various booths, which open up onto the square, where coffee and tobacco may be consumed. The benches of these rooms are arranged in the form of an amphitheatre, and in the middle of such a place stands a basin of fresh water, which one requires for filling the pipe with water, when the same becomes over-heated from the tobacco smoke. All Persians, or those of them in possession of money, never fail to gather at such places every day between seven and eight in the morning, upon which they are promptly served with a pipe, and a bowl of coffee.

But the great Shah Abas, seeing that such places provided at the same time opportunity for gatherings for the purpose of discussing affairs of state, a fact which occasioned his displeasure, he resolved, in order to prevent the minor mutinies, which could thereby be engendered the following instruction: He introduced the custom that every morning before anyone entered such a place, a *mullah* should go to each of these booths, and engage the coffee drinkers and tobacco smokers in instruction on some aspect of their laws, or on history, or poetry. And this custom . . . is still practised today.

Turkish Coffee

A long-handled pot called an *ibrik* is essential in making true Turkish coffee. The *ibrik* has a tapering brass or copper shape and no cover. The coffee used in it must be finely pulverized into a powder and of a dark roast.

Following the Chinese tradition, the Arabs use small china cups that have no handles, and have devised small metal holders (*zarfs*) of brass, silver, or copper, ornately etched or carved to match serving trays. True Turkish coffee cups are barely the size of an eggshell and do not have *zarfs*. The cups are frequently cylindrical rather than round, and very small, with the capacity to hold about two ounces at most.

To make true Turkish coffee, measure four tablespoons of the pulverized coffee to one and one-half cups of water and four teaspoons of sugar; combine in the pot. Never fill the pot more than one-half to two-thirds its capacity. Bring the combination to boiling over a medium heat, then remove from the heat until the froth subsides.

Repeat the procedure two more times, allowing the froth to settle each time.

Remove the pot from the heat on the third time and spoon some of the creamy foam into each cup. Fill each cup but do not stir. Demitasse cups will do, but should only be two-thirds filled.

In Arabic the word for the creamy foam (*wesh*) is translated as the "face of the coffee," and to serve it without the foam is to "lose face."

"In the Levant it is only the scum of the people who swallow the grounds," said Dr. Sylvestre Dufour, whose contribution to coffee legend and fact consists of the first serious analysis of coffee and the first identification of the odorless, bitter alkaloid in coffee known as caffeine. Considering that his report was written in the seventeenth century, about 1685, this is quite a remarkable discovery, and we can pardon his attitude about Turkish coffee.

In the Middle East, coffee drinking remains an important social activity both in the cafés, where telling jokes, riddles, and tales is not uncommon, and playing backgammon (*tric-trac*) and charades is enjoyed by all. Coffee is never served during business or bargaining.

In the Middle East the Turkish *ibrik* is referred to as a *tanaka* and holds from one to five cups of coffee.

Coffee-drinking etiquette is strictly regulated, with the person of highest rank served first, then the oldest, and with men usually being served before women, although that is changing. One is always asked the strength of sweetness desired, and each visitor is served freshly brewed coffee from freshly roasted and pulverized beans, prepared as you arrive.

THE MIDDLE EAST

Egyptian Coffee

In Egypt, coffee is served at occasions happy and sad. It is not uncommon to serve unsweetened coffee to mourners at funerals and sweetened coffee at weddings, to demonstrate sorrow and joy at the respective events. In his nineteenth-century book *The Manners and Customs of the Modern Egyptians*, author William Lane gave a more detailed account of coffee making in Egypt (*qahweh* is coffee; *bababan* is cardamon; ambergris is a waxy substance that comes from sperm whales' digestive tracts and is used as a perfume additive; and mastic is a pasty material used to coat cement):

> The *qahweh* is made very strong, and without sugar or milk. The *finggan* [cup] is small, generally holding not quite an ounce and a half of liquid. It is of porcelain, or Dutch-ware, and being without a handle, is placed within a *zarf* of silver or brass, according to the circumstances of the owner, and, both in shape and size, nearly resembling an egg cup. In preparing the coffee, the water is first made to boil: the freshly roasted and pounded coffee is then put in, and stirred;

after which the pot is again placed on the fire, once or twice until the coffee begins to simmer; when it is taken off and its contents are poured out into the cups while the surface [of the coffee] is yet creamy (*kaymagh*).

The Egyptians are excessively fond of pure and strong coffee thus prepared; and very seldom add sugar to it and never milk or cream; but a little *hababan* seed is often added to it. It is a common custom, also to fumigate the cup with the smoke of *mastic* and the wealthy sometimes impregnate the coffee with the delicious fragrance of ambergris. The most general mode of doing this is to put about a carat-weight of ambergris in a coffee pot, and melt it over a fire; then make the coffee in another pot in the manner before described and when it has settled a little, pour it into the pot which contains the ambergris. Some persons make use of the ambergris, for the same purpose in a different way; sticking a piece of it, of the weight of about two carats in the bottom of a cup and then pouring in the coffee; a piece of the weight above mentioned will serve for two or three weeks. This mode is often adopted by persons who like always to have the coffee which they themselves drink flavoured with the perfume, and do not give all their visitors the same luxury.

Bedouin Coffee

The Bedouins often use coffee that is half roasted, resulting in a very mild, weak brew frequently only forty percent coffee to sixty percent cardamom, a popular flavoring that imparts to the coffee a yellowish color and sweetish taste, although no sugar or honey is used. Sometimes Bedouins add ginger instead of the cardamom, and this style of mild, flavored coffee can be found in Syria, Turkey, Yemen, and Jedda in Saudi Arabia, especially in their popular cafés.

In the Bedouin home, coffee is generally served plain, with ginger or cardamom served after the brewing as condiments for guests to use as they desire. To be a guest in a Bedouin home is quite an honor, and traditional hosts offer a classic version of pure Bedouin hospitality, centered around coffee preparation.

A guest would most likely be greeted by the host saying, *"Ahlah wa Sahlan,"* "My home is your home." As part of this elaborate ceremony, customized furniture accessories are brought out from a special chest used solely for this purpose. Your host will roast the fresh beans himself in a long-handled cast iron ladle, keeping the beans moving with a long iron stirrer to assure an even roast. The beans are then allowed to cool in a shallow bowl, and then hand-ground with a brass mortar by the host in a quick, almost musical, rhythm. To say a Bedouin "pounds coffee from morning to night" is a great compliment, for he is a host who is generous and entertains often.

The host's eldest son will serve you, offering a handleless cup from those stacked in the palm of his right hand. With his left hand, the son will pour the coffee from a long-spouted brass pot. Sugar is not unheard of, but is boiled at the same time as the coffee. Guests can be asked ahead of time their preference: *belou*, sweet; *mazbout*, medium; or *murra*, unsweetened. Important guests are served first, and others are served according to their seniority. In some areas it is the host who is served first to make sure that the pot is not spoiled or, heaven forbid, deadly.

As a guest, you have a role to play as well: You take and hold the half-filled tiny cup in your right hand, accepting one to three cups. Cups are always only half filled, for a filled one would be an insult, as if to say "Fill the cup for an enemy" or, worse, "Drink up and leave."

When you are finished, you extend your cup to the server, rotating it by moving your wrist, not your arm. To say "I am finished, that's all," you say the words *khalass* or *bass*. In response the host will say, "Go in God's safekeeping." *(For a more detailed rendition of this ceremony, see below under Coffee in the K'hawah.)*

Coffee in Arabia

The first cup is for the guest, the second for enjoyment, the third for the sword.
—old Arabic saying

Coffee and hospitality are practically the same thing in Arab countries, and the Arabic coffee-brewing method can certainly be called the "true" one. Although it is usually served thick and black, powdered cloves, cracked cardamom seed, or powdered cinnamon can be added, after which the brew is returned to the heat to boil up to three times.

It is not uncommon to see hosts rinse the tiny cups by pouring some fresh hot coffee from one cup to another to heat them, although this warming coffee is then poured on the ground to honor the saint of coffee, Sheik ash-Shadhili.

O Coffee, thou dispersest sorrow;
Thou are the drink of the faithful,
Thou givest health to those who labor,
And enablest the good to find the truth.
—Sheik Abd el Kader

COFFEE IN THE K'HAWAH

One of the most appealing stories of the ancient Arab coffee ceremony was described by William Palgrave in his detailed book, *Narrative of a Year's Journey*:

The *K'hawah* was a large oblong hall, about twenty feet in height, fifty in length and sixteen or thereabouts, in breadth; the walls were coloured in a rudely decorative manner with brown and white wash, and sunk here and there into small triangular recesses, destined to be the reception of books, though of these Ghafil at least had no overabundance, lamps, and other such objects. The roof of timber, and flat; the floor was strewed with fine clean sand, and garnished all around alongside of the walls with long strips of carpet, upon which cushions, covered with faded silk, were disposed at suitable intervals. In poorer houses felt rugs usually take the place of carpets.

In one corner, namely, that furthest removed from the door, stood a small fireplace, or, to speak more exactly, furnace, formed of a large square block of granite, or some other hard stone, about twenty inches each way; this is hollowed inwardly into a deep funnel, open above, and communicating below with a small horizontal tube or pipe-hole, through which the air passes, bellows-driven, to the lighted charcoal piled up on a grating about half-way inside the cone. In this manner the fuel is soon brought to a white heat, and the water in the coffee-pot placed upon the funnel's mouth is readily brought to boil. The system of coffee furnaces is universal in Djowf and Djebel Shomer, but in Nejed itself, and indeed in whatever other yet more distant regions of Arabia I visited to the south and east, the furnace is replaced by an open fireplace hollowed in the ground floor, with a raised stone border, and dog-irons for the fuel, and so forth, like what may be yet seen in Spain. This diversity of arrangement, so far as Arabia is concerned, is due to the greater abundance of fire-wood in the south, whereby the inhabitants are enabled to light up on a larger scale; whereas throughout the Djowf and Djebel Shomer wood is very scarce, and the only fuel at hand is bad charcoal, often brought from a considerable distance, and carefully husbanded.

This corner of the *K'hawah* is also the place of distinction whence honour and coffee radiate by progressive degrees round the apartment, and hereabouts accordingly sits the master of the house himself, or the guests whom he more especially delights to honour.

On the broad edge of the furnace or fireplace, as the case may be, stands an ostentatious range of copper coffee-pots, varying in size and form. Here in the Djowf the coffee-pot they make resembles that in vogue at Damascus; but in Nejed and the eastern districts they are of a different and much more ornamental fashioning, very tall and slender, with several ornamental circles and mouldings in elegant relief, besides boasting long beak-shaped spouts and high steeples for covers. The number of these utensils is often extravagantly great. I have seen a dozen at a time in a row by one fireside, though coffee-making requires, in fact, only three at most. Here in the Djowf five or six are considered to be the thing; for the south this number must be doubled; all this to indicate the riches and munificence of their owner, but implying the frequency of his guests and the large amount of coffee that he is in consequence obliged to have made for them.

Behind this stove sits, at least in wealthy houses, a black slave, whose name is generally a diminutive in token of familiarity or affection; in the recent case it was Soweylim, the diminutive of Salim. His occupation is to make and pour out the coffee; where there is no slave in the family, the master of the premises himself, or perhaps one of his sons, performs that hospitable duty; rather a tedious one, as we shall soon see.

We enter. On passing the threshold it is proper to say, *"Bismillah,"* i.e., "in the name of God"; not to do so would be looked on as a bad augury alike for him who enters and for those within. The visitor next advances in silence, till on coming about half-way across the room, he gives to all present, but looking specially at the master of the house, the customary *"Essalamu' aleykum"* or "Peace be with you," literally, "on you." All this while every one else in the room has kept his place, motionless, and without saying a word. But on receiving the *salaam* of etiquette, the master of the house rises, and if a strict Wahhabee, or at any rate desirous of seeming such, replies with the full-length traditonary formula, *"Waleykumu-s-salamu, w'rabmat' Ullabi w'barakatub,"* which is, as everyone knows, "And with (or, on) you be peace, and the mercy of God, and his blessings." But should he happen to be of anti-Wahhabee tendencies the odds are that he will say *"Marhba,"* or *"Ablan w' sablan,"* i.e., "welcome" or "worthy, and pleasurable," or the like; for of such phrases there is an infinite, but elegant variety.

All present follow the example thus given, by rising and saluting. The guest then goes up to the master of the house, who has also made a step or two forwards, and places his open hand in the palm of his host's, but without grasping or shaking, which would hardly pass for decorous, and at the same time each repeats once more his greeting, followed by the set phrases of polite enquiry. "How are you?" "How goes the world with you?" and so forth, all in a tone of great interest, and to be gone over three or four times, till one or other has the discretion to say *"El hamdu l'illah,"* "Praise be to God," or, in equivalent value, "all right," and this is a signal for a diversion to the ceremonious interrogatory.

The guest then, after a little contest of courtesy, takes his seat in the honoured post by the fireplace, after an apologetical salutation to the black slave on the one side, and to his nearest neighbour on the other. The best cushions and newest looking carpets have been of course prepared for his honoured weight. Shoes or sandals, for in truth the latter alone are used in Arabia, are slipped off on the sand just before reaching the carpet, and they remain on the floor close by. But the riding stick or wand, the inseparable companion of every true Arab, whether Bedouin or townsman, rich or poor, gentle or simple, is to be retained in the hand, and will serve for playing with during the pauses of conversation, like the fan of our great-grandmothers in their days of conquest.

Without delay Soweylim begins his preparations for coffee. These open by about five minutes of blowing with the bellows and arranging the charcoal till a sufficient heat has been produced. Next he places the largest of the coffeepots, a huge machine, and about two-thirds full of clear water, close by the edge of the glowing coal-pit, that its contents may become gradually warm while other operations are in progress. He then takes a dirty knotted rag out of a niche in the wall close by and having untied it, empties out of it three or four handfuls of unroasted coffee, which he places on a little trencher of platted grass, and picks carefully out any blackened grains, or other non-homologous substances, commonly to be found intermixed with the berries when purchased in gross; then, after much cleansing and shaking, he pours the grain so cleansed into a large open iron ladle, and places it over the mouth of the funnel, at the same time blow-

ing the bellows and stirring the grains gently round and round till they crackle, redden, and smoke a little, but carefully withdrawing them from the heat long before they turn black or charred, after the erroneous fashion of Turkey and Europe; after which he puts them to cool a moment on the grass platter.

He then sets the warm water in the large coffee-pot over the fire aperture, that it may be ready boiling at the right moment, and draws in close between his own trouserless legs a large stone mortar, with a narrow pit in the middle, just enough to admit the large stone pestle of a foot long and an inch and a half thick, which he now takes in hand. Next, pouring the half-roasted berries into the mortar, he proceeds to pound them, striking right into the narrow hollow with wonderful dexterity, nor ever missing his blow till the beans are smashed, but not reduced into powder. He then scoops them out, now reduced to a sort of coarse reddish grit, very unlike the fine charcoal dust which passes in some countries for coffee, and out of which every particle of real aroma has long since been burnt or ground.

After all these operations, each performed with as intense a seriousness and deliberate nicety as if the welfare of the entire Djowf depended on it, he takes a smaller coffee-pot in hand, fills it more than half with hot water from the larger vessel, and then shaking the pounded coffee into it, sets it on the fire to boil, occasionally stirring it with a small stick as the water rises to check the ebullition and prevent overflowing. Nor should the boiling stage to be long or vehement; on the contrary, it is and should be as light as possible. In the interim he takes out of another rag-knot a few aromatic seeds called heyl, an Indian product, but of whose scientific name I regret to be wholly ignorant, or a little saffron, and after slightly pounding these ingredients, throws them into the simmering coffee to improve its flavour, for such an additional spicing is held indispensable in Arabia though often omitted elsewhere in the East. Sugar would be a totally unheard of profanation. Last of all, he strains off the liquor through some fibres of the inner palm-bar placed for that purpose in the jug-spout, and gets ready the tray of delicate coloured grass, and the small coffee cups ready for pouring out. All these preliminaries have taken up a good half-hour.

Today, this elaborate "ceremonious interrogatory" would be reduced considerably, but in the Middle East, where hospitality is akin to breathing, coffee is still made as soon as a guest arrives, and to refuse a host's offer of coffee would be unforgivable.

BOSNIA AND HERZEGOVINA

A COFFEE MOMENT

Diane Kordick, Sebastopol, California

I visited what was then Yugoslavia in 1986, the birthplace of my father's parents and my mother's grandparents. It was a very nostalgic trip for me, and I cher-

ish the memories of my only chance to visit relatives and see the beautiful countryside of my heritage country, particularly Bosnia and Herzegovina. I especially adored visiting Dubrovnik, the spectacular walled city in Croatia that faces
the Adriatic Sea, with a view to Italy. It is a city where one walks, and soaks up
the sounds and sights of hundreds of years of fine history and culture.

I am not normally a coffee drinker, but in Yugoslavia one stops by the local
kafano every few hours to get a fix of coffee as if it were medicine. Despite all
the many cups I drank, I don't ever recall being buzzed like mediocre coffee in
a Styrofoam cup does to me here in the States. We would sit among all the
older men lounging around and talking Serbo-Croatian in the *kafanos*, usually
crudely built open-air coffeehouses. The small *kafanos* were usually run by the
owner, who would take your order, brew the coffee, and serve as well. When
we visited our relatives, it was the wife who brewed and served, and she stood
continuously, always at the ready to refill our cups, quite a shock to this West-
ern woman.

Coffee both at homes and in the *kafanos* was served in a long-handled open
pot, a *dezva* (pronounced "jezva") and the coffee was poured into tiny demitasse-
style cups. The locals would knock back the coffee quickly, but this was an
experience totally new to me, so I drank the thick, sweet coffee slowly and
enjoyed it enormously. As we drove along the countryside stopping at one *selo*
(village) after another, I marveled at the beauty of my family's homeland and
gained a more intimate understanding of how my parents were raised and how
this heritage affected them as children and grandchildren of Croatian immi-
grants to America. The memory of that trip is all the more poignant when I
realize that the divisiveness that changed kingdoms of the Austrian-Hungarian
Empire into states following the First World War is happening again as these
states declare their independence one after another from what has been known
as Yugoslavia.

✧✧✧

GREECE

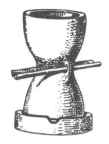

The *briki*, a version of the Arabian *ibrik*, is the coffeemaker of choice in Greece, where the coffee is hot and thick and sweet. Traditional Greek pastries, with their honey, almonds, and pistachios, have long been the perfect accompaniment to such strong coffee.

The creamy foam that results from this style of coffee making is as critical to the Greeks as it is to Middle Eastern coffee traditions. In Greek coffee lore, young Greek girls would use this as a silent but powerful signal to suitors and husbands. When suitors came to call, a young Greek girl would serve coffee with foam (*karmake*) if she thought the suitor was marriage material; without the foam if she wished to silently convey her rejection. After marriage a woman could tell her husband that she was upset with him by pouring his coffee without the foam. This ritual can be used to say much more than some of the elaborate communications "techniques" we employ today.

In Greece one visits the *kafe* or *kafeneia*, but there, as in many Middle Eastern countries, you will find an audience of men only. You can order your coffee in various degrees of sweetness: *metrios vrastos*, boiled medium with a half teaspoon of sugar; *vays glykos*, strong yet sweet, with one teaspoon of sugar; and *glykos vrastos*, very sweet with about 1½ teaspoons of sugar. (Each of these variations has the same amount of coffee.) If you're really a purist, you could order it *sketos*, with no sugar at all.

Greeks tell fortunes by reading patterns in coffee grounds; look for a big blob, which means money, but watch out for little blobs, they spell trouble. Widely spaced grounds could mean a long trip; grounds together, short trips, probably to the coffee merchant for more beans.

FRANCE

Good coffee is more than a savory cup,
Its aroma has the power to dry liquor up,

By coffee you get upon leaving the table
A mind full of wisdom, thoughts lucid, nerves stable;
And odd tho' it be, 'tis none the less true,
Coffee's aid to digestion permits dining anew.
And what's very true, tho' few people know it,
Fine coffee's the basis of every fine poet;
For many a writer as windy as Boreas
Has been vastly improved by the drink ever glorious

—excerpted from an eighteenth-century
French poem, author unknown

Sipping coffee at cafes along the boulevards of Paris or at various squares in the City of Light is a must for the traveler and native alike. But sophisticated Parisians did not originate this tradition; credit goes instead to traders in the provinces, particularly the seaport of Marseilles.

Merchants from Marseilles traveled widely in the Levant, bringing home their treasured coffee beans. They joined forces with druggists to import coffee in bales of beans from Egypt, with eager entrepreneurs in Lyons following suit.

Suleiman Agai, an ambassador of Sultan Muhommad IV of Turkey, arrived in Paris in 1669 to serve at the court of Louis XIV and learn state secrets to carry home with him. He brought to the French court great mountains of coffee beans and entertained the court with great ceremony serving this "amber beverage." He quickly learned that the relaxed state induced in the courtiers by his coffee ceremonies was perfect for loosening tongues and revealing information he'd been sent to glean.

Suleiman Aga's showmanship involved "importing" to the French court black slaves, the taller and larger the better for their dramatic presence, always dressed in turbans and lavish sky blue robes. In the regal rooms of the palace, these slaves, theatrically costumed and with great flourish, would serve Arab-style coffee in fragile

eggshell porcelain cups displayed on gold and silver saucers. The court guests were handed embroidered silk doilies on which to place the beautiful saucers that held the tiny cups of the exotic brew. This sumptuous form of entertainment set off a years-long fad of everything Turkish in Paris.

This trend to the Turkish was further amplified when the Armenian, Pascal, capitalized on the aura of the exotic coffee. He first came to Paris in 1672, setting up a tent at the Fair of St. Germain, where he hung pots of coffee on spirit lamps and the smell of his *petit noir* wafted through the area, drawing Frenchmen to his place. He sent out coffee waiters, *garçons du café*, often young Turks he had wangled into Paris, to attract people further. For three sous, a pittance, the Frenchmen could luxuriate in surroundings in the style that only the nobility had previously enjoyed. Pascal's copy of Constantinople coffeehouses, his own *maison du café*, was spectacularly successful, and he took his art later to London to huge success.

A cup of coffee detracts nothing from your intellect; on the contrary, your stomach is freed by it and no longer distresses your brain; it will not hamper your mind with troubles but give freedom to its working . . . work becomes easier and you will sit down without distress to your principal repast which will restore your body and afford you a calm delicious night.

—Talleyrand

The first true Parisian coffeehouse, Café Procope, was opened in 1689 by a former *limonadier* (lemonade vendor), François Procope (a Sicilian by birth, he was also known by his Italian name, Procopio dei Costelli). The luxurious café had marble tables, chandeliers, paintings, and large gilt mirrors, doing much to persuade the French bourgeoisie from wines and spirits and into the coffeehouse. Its location, at 13 rue de l'Ancienne-Comédie, could not have been more enticing, facing the Théâtre Français, where it drew the *artistes* and *auteurs* of the day: Rousseau, Diderot, Beaumarchais, and later, during the Revolution, Marat, Robespierre, and Danton. By 1720 Paris was home to 380 garden and sidewalk cafés, and by 1870, there were 3,000; no smaller number of them are in business today. Café Procope, which still exists, was also the scene of the first French ice cream parlor, but that's another story.

Honoré de Balzac, who often drank twenty to thirty cups of coffee per day, recorded his great appreciation for coffee in his *Treatise on Modern Stimulants*, including this passage: "The coffee falls into your stomach, and straightaway there is a general commotion. Ideas begin to move like battalions of the Grand Army battlefield, and the battle takes place. . . . Similes arise, the paper is covered with ink; for the struggle commences and is included with torrents of black water, just as battle with powder."

Flaubert viewed coffee, particularly black coffee, as a fashionable beverage. "Take it without sugar," he counseled, "very swank."

Although the French make their coffee in many ways, it is most typically infused. Following the principle of the Colombian *cafezhine* or Costa Rican sock method, the French began making coffee *sans ebullition* (without boiling) in 1711. They filled a cloth bag with the grounds, dropped it inside a coffeepot, and poured boiling water over it. Of course, it was and is difficult to keep the bag clean this way, and it should be washed and left in fresh water until it is used again. The Costa Ricans simply rinse it clear of grounds and hang it up on the wall to dry, as do the Colombians.

Le Café, a French periodical of the mid 1800s, had as its slogan, "The salon stood for privilege, the café stands for equality." Perhaps that is why coffee is often referred to as the drink of democracy. As evidence, after the cafés came to Paris, they became the centers of political commentary—and contention. The infamous French revolution was born in French cafés. Giving direct birth to this ferment was journalist Camille Desmoulins who, working himself into an oratorical frenzy, began his litany in Café Foi in 1789. Spurred on by Desmoulins's verbal campaign, Parisians took to the streets and two days later the Bastille fell, marking the overthrow of the French government and changing France forever.

In 1895 the Lumière brothers of France premiered their first film at the Indian Salon of the Grand Café in Paris. Showing films quickly became another way to draw people into the coffeehouses of France, Germany, and other European countries.

Coffee has come into general use as a food in the morning, and after dinner as an exhilarating and tonic drink.

—Jean Anthelme Brillat-Savarin, *The Physiology of Taste*

Café Momus and Café Rotonde became the center of the artistic and literary movements that enlivened the Latin Quarter of Henri de Toulouse-Lautrec and, several decades later, of the Lost Generation of Ernest Hemingway and F. Scott Fitzgerald. Parisian cafés became places to see and be seen, to flaunt lovers, wallow in the black cup, and thus avoid the empty canvas or blank sheet of paper—or at least to be positively witty about those who could be rightfully called *artistes*.

Music came to the coffeehouse with the *café chanteuse*, of whom one of the most popular was the soprano Rosalba. Accompanied by blind musicians, she entertained patrons until past midnight. Both male and female singers and a variety of musicians transformed the more modest cafés into *cafés chantants*, and *chanson* societies were formed everywhere. The repertoire was based on the issue of the day, satirical *ballades* against the aristocracy during the French Revolution and the satires against the Jacobins at places patronized by the upper classes. Between 1789 and 1794 more than 3,000 *chansons* were composed, an integral part of the revolution and its propaganda. The *cafés chantants* were banned periodically, depending on who was then in the government. The entertainment evolved into small orchestras for *café concerts*, and then such luminaries of passion as Edith Piaf, Yves Montand, and Charles Aznavour carried on the tradition through the forties and fifties.

T R A I T E Z
Nouveaux & curieux

DU CAFE',
DU THE'
ET DU
CHOCOLATE.
Ouvrage également neceſſaire aux
Medecins, & à tous ceux qui
aiment leur ſanté.

Par PHILIPPE SYLVESTRE DUFOUR

A quoy on a adjoûté dans cette Edition, la meil-
leure de toutes les methodes, qui manquoit
à ce Livre, pour compoſer

L'EXCELLENT CHOCOLATE.
Par Mr. St. DISDIER.
Troiſiéme Edition.

A LA HAYE,
Chez ADRIAN MOETJENS, Mar-
chand Libraire prez la Cour, à la
Libraire Françoiſe.

M. DC. XCIII.

✧✧✧

A liquid there is to the poet most dear,
'Twas lacking to Virgil, adored by Voltaire,
'Tis though, divine coffee, for thine is the art,
Without turning the head yet to gladden the heart.
　　　—from *Divine Coffee,* by Jacques Delille
　　　　(1738-1815), translated from the French

SCANDINAVIA

A COFFEE MOMENT

Virginia Williams Lusk, Mill Valley,
California

My partner and I arrived in Sweden from London via a wonderful trip on the overnight ferryboat. We were both excited about our new business venture, developing the Norwegian salmon market for Northern California, and I was looking forward to being the English-Swedish translator for the seafood company we had created, plus pursuing my design studies at the University of Gothenburg.

It was summer, and very warm for Sweden, nearly 75 degrees, as we took the clanging streetcar to downtown Gothenburg. We decided on dinner at a very small café, a rustic mom-and-pop kind of place. Everything was fabulous. We had an unbelievably delicious halibut caught that very morning and served with fresh grated horseradish and incredible side dishes; it was simply the perfect meal. I did not think anything could top it, when the waiter brought us these very tiny, old-fashioned Dansk-style cups with small handles on their sides. I remember taking that first sip and the taste was so delicious, so strong, I literally thought my teeth would pop out. The coffee tasted so rich; it was thick as syrup, but not at all bitter. I had never tasted anything like it. This was my first understanding of what a fulfilling cup could be, excellent and enough, you could not possibly have another cup.

As I extended my stay in Sweden, I got used to this divine drink and sometimes had more than one cup, but none was ever as incredible, as shocking, or as satisfying as that first sip of Swedish coffee in downtown Gothenburg on a hot summer's eve.

While we cannot be certain that what our contributor had was *grug*, a popular Scandinavian coffee common to the villages, it was certainly a variation of it. *Grug* is made in an open copper kettle filled with water into which coarse ground coffee is added; the mixture is boiled down until thick. The people of Norway, Sweden, and Denmark are all big coffee drinkers, and each country has its own method for making dark rich coffee.

ITALY

They sit at their meat (which is served to them on the ground as tailors sit upon their stalls, cross-legged); for the most part, passing the day in banqueting and carowsing [sic], until they surfet, drinking a certain liquor, which they do call coffe [sic].
    —Anthony Sherley, 1565–1636 following
     a visit from Venice to Persia on which
     he observed Turks partaking of their
     favorite drink

It is hard to imagine an Italy without coffee, but for years the beverages of choice were wine and, believe it or not, lemonade. It was fear of competition that led Italian lemonade vendors and wine merchants in the late 1600s to stage a campaign against coffee. The merchants, using the now familiar routine of labeling coffee the brew of the Devil, pleaded with Pope Clement VII to issue an edict that coffee was unholy or unworthy. Confident that the Pope was on their side, the merchants were astonished at the result. The Pope, not one to rush to judgment, resisted issuing an immediate indictment and, instead, asked to taste this exotic beverage. Far from being repulsed, he was overwhelmingly delighted with its taste and aroma.

"Why, this Satan's drink is so delicious," he is alleged to have said, "it would be a pity to let the infidels have exclusive use of it. We shall fool Satan by baptizing it and making it a truly Christian beverage."

The Pope did indeed fully baptize the new beverage, which led to an ironically long and still vibrant coffee history in Italy, home of espresso, caffè latte, and the rest.

Pope Clement VII was not the only pontiff to wax rhapsodic about coffee. Pope Leo XII wrote, when he was eighty-eight, a short ode to the brew in *Frugality*:

> *Last comes the beverage of the Orient shore,*
> *Mocha, far off, the fragrant berries bore.*
> *Taste the dark fluid with a dainty lip,*
> *Digestion waits on pleasure as you sip.*

The Venetians were the first to import coffee to Europe, most probably about 1615, and at that time it was called not coffee but, after the direct meaning of the Arabic word *qhaweh*, "the wine of Arabia." It was the Venetians who capitalized on their merchant relationship with the Arabs, loading their "brown gold" treasures in Mocha and taking the Mocha-Venice route to the Italian city.

It was not just the traders who espoused the virtues and delights of this new beverage, but men of letters as well. Prospero Alpino had exclaimed its virtues as early as

1592 with his treatise *De Plantis Aegypti* (The Plant of Egypt), and Pietro della Valle, a seventeenth-century man of letters, wrote extensively on coffee and its many benefits. But, as it was in the Middle East before them, it was the coffeehouse once again that was the direct link between the promoters of coffee and the end-use consumer. As with all things Italian, the coffeehouse in Rome and Venice and other famous spots was done with a decidedly lavish style. It is certainly a testament to these early interior designers and architects that nearly three hundred years later many of these coffeehouses still exist.

Many Italian coffeehouses are often now stand-up bars suitable for a quick jolt of espresso (the word espresso means "expressly for you"). The fine sit-down cafés that still exist are places to take your time, ogle the pretty people, read the *International Herald-Tribune*, or socialize with friends, new and old.

Despite its longevity, the coffeehouse did not happen overnight. It would be several decades before the strolling lemonade vendors would allow the first coffeehouse to be opened along the canals of Venice. Even then, they were first called *botteghe del acque e dei ghiaccio*, "cafés that serve drinks made with water and ice." Sometime between 1647 and 1683 (historians differ) the *botteghe del caffè* finally won over the lemonade vendors, and Venice had its first true coffeehouse.

Perhaps the most famous of these Venetian coffeehouses was Floriano Francescone's Caffè della Venezia Trionfante, named to honor (or placate) the rulers of that era. Francescone later changed the name to his own, and it became what it is known today as Caffè Florian. The interior is divided into small rooms: dei Quadri, del Senato, Greek, and Chinese, full of the best of Italian art. There is tinted stucco work, fresco paintings (some by Carlini) and gold inlay everywhere among the small tables of wood and marble. The historic café has undergone much renovation over the nearly two and one half centuries of its existence, but still evokes the era of its birth.

It faces St. Mark's Square (Piazza San Marco), as it has since it opened in 1720, and rests under the arcade of the Procuratie Nuove. Its main rival, the Caffe Quadri, faces it on the other side, and in summertime the piazza is filled with patrons from both cafés who sit upon the spindly little chairs and bask in the sun, with the beautiful cathedral and the views of the palazzi all around the square to enchant them while

drinking their *caffès*. Caffè Florian was just the beginning. With art reflecting life, Carlo Goldoni wrote about this new phenomenon in his comedy *La Bottega del Caffè* in 1750, and that popular theater piece helped to fuel the enthusiasm for this new style of socializing, so that by 1759 Venice alone had more than 206 cafés.

Before one could say double *caffè latte*, coffeehouses spread to Florence and Genoa, with many more sprouting up throughout the main cities of Italy. Mornings were given over to the working men en route to their jobs, and the leisure class took over in the afternoons and long into the evenings. For a while coffeehouses served as both barber shops and gambling houses, but they soon gave way for pure coffee pleasures and socializing.

Coffee was promoted in the literary and philosophical journal *Il Caffè*, named after the setting in which the publisher and his friends discussed issues of the day. The newspaper was only published briefly, from June of 1764 to May of 1766, by intellectuals belonging to the Accademia dei Pugni, among them brothers Pietro and Alessandro Verri with Cesare Beccaria. This short-lived journal has remained the benchmark publication and symbol of the type of intellectual activity that coffeehouses encouraged. It was the place where men "discussed the spirit of Italian letters" and provided moral analysis of society for one another. Caffè Florian also was the scene for much political commentary, including the founding of still another famous newspaper, Gaspare Gazzi's *Gazzetta Veneta*.

For a while lemonade and coffee continued to be sold together, and both gained in popularity because of another new product, sugar. (Before the eighteenth-century, honey was the universal sweetener.) Although most lemonade vendors resisted this new beverage, one of the most famous vendors, Antonio Pedrocchi (1776–1852) saw the future and made the simple café he inherited from his father Francesco into a splendid temple of coffee. He was aided by the drama contributed by the skilled architect Giuseppe Jappeli. Renovated in 1831, Pedrocchi's café became one of the most beautiful coffeehouses in Italy. Even today one can step up for an espresso at its gracious carved marble bar on the ground floor or pick from one of ten differently decorated rooms upstairs in which to have an assignation or business meeting or simply to sip one's coffee alone with the newspaper.

Throughout the lasting novels and reportage of Italy during these years, we read of such famous poetic-sounding coffeehouse names as Gambrinus in Naples; Pedrocchi in Padua; Fiori, Platti, Fiorio, Baratti, Milano, and San Carlo in Turin; Tommaseo and San Marco in Trieste; Greco and Aragno in Rome; and Michelangelo in Florence—all of which were the esteemed literary salons of their era.

A COFFEE MOMENT

Richard-Thomas, San Anselmo, California

I was stationed at a U.S. Air Force base in Aviano, Italy, a small, quiet community nestled serenely against the eastern Dolomites. Being an SP [Security Policeman] this was more meditative than cops-and-robbers. Even so, I relished the opportunity to be off the base. One day I boarded the train for the one-and-a-half-hour trip to Venice, arriving as the long shadows of dusk enveloped the famous Venetian canals. As I stepped off the train, Venice lay before me, more wonderful than any photograph could depict. I walked from the train under the Victorian ironwork of the dramatic station through its grand lobby, with its murky marble, darkened art deco furnishings, and glass doorways marking the entrance into the Venetian twilight.

The sounds and smells of this old train station surrounded me as I stepped up to the burnished brass bar with its copper counters, setting one of my boot-clad feet upon the brass railing and ordering a cappuccino. It was perfect. The hot bittersweet coffee flavor came through the frothy milk; it was a taste like no other.

I walked out into the revelry of Carnivale in Venice. Unlike its garish sisters in Rio de Janeiro and New Orleans, the Venetian version of Carnivale is theater with all its mystery, and a pure magic I have not felt or seen since.

Austria

*When you are worried, have trouble of one sort
or another—to the coffeehouse!
When she did not keep her appointment, for
one reason or other—to the coffeehouse!
When your shoes are torn and dilapidated—
coffeehouse!
When your income is four hundred crowns and
you spend five hundred—coffeehouse!
You are a chair warmer in some office, while
your ambition led you to seek professional
honors—coffeehouse!
You could not find a mate to suit you—
coffeehouse!
You feel like committing suicide—coffeehouse!
You hate and despise human beings, and at the
same time you cannot be happy without
them—coffeehouse!*

—from "To the Coffeehouse,"
by Peter Altenberg, Viennese poet

Some might say coffee's entry into Vienna was an international ploy. Muhammad IV sent his men from Constantinople in 1683 and they quickly surrounded Vienna, cutting it off from the rest of the world. While the 300,000 Turkish soldiers kept the armies of the Duke of Lorraine and King John of Poland—friendly to Vienna—at bay, one Franz Georg Kolschitzky donned an ornate Turkish uniform and made his way through enemy lines several times, providing communications that led to the friendly armies' sending the Turks back to Constantinople.

Kolschitzky, a Pole who had lived in the East for years, watched the fleeing Turkish troops which left Vienna with 25,000 tents, 10,000 oxen, 5,000 camels, and a large quantity of gold. One of the things the Turks left behind were coffee beans, hastily thrown on the bonfire but promptly noticed by Kolschitzky as a whiff from his past. He saved the beans from the flames, wrangled the right to cart them away, and opened Vienna's first coffeehouse, the Blue Bottle (or the Blue Flask), which spawned an official guild of others, which were called *kaffe-sieder*, or coffeemakers.

Viennese pastries have accompanied millions of cups of coffee, and this exquisite category of desserts is worth a separate book. For the purposes of our story, two confections that are tied to this part of Austria's history demand description: *kipfel* and *krapfen*.

Kipfel is a pastry that began as an act of defiance: it was and still is baked in the shape of the crescent of the Turkish flag. *Krapfen*, a pastry commissioned by Kolschitzky himself, is known today as the jelly doughnut. These two famous desserts, and legions of other Austrian tortes, petit fours, cookies, and cakes, are sweet accompaniments to strongly brewed coffee served in one of three variations: *mélange*, coffee with milk; *braun*, darker than *mélange* but lighter than *schwarzer*, which is black and very strong.

It was during Kolschitzky's time that the tradition of coffeehouses welcoming radicals, anarchists, artists, and poets began in Vienna, and it continued well into the twentieth century. The coffee lover is fortunate to have many famous cafés to enjoy today, like Café Schwarzenberg and Central Café, although some of the most extraordinary have disappeared, like the legendary Silberkammer.

The Silberkammer (Silbernes Kaffeehaus) which opened in Vienna in 1824 and lasted for nearly twenty-five years, had as its benchmark absolute luxury. Everything that could be made of real silver was: from the unexpected, like the coat hooks and door handles, to the more obvious pots, cups, and spoons. Only the finest and most expensive woods were used for the billiard tables and wainscoting. It was unrestrained sumptuousness all around, a true homage to coffee and the patrons who enjoyed this new beverage.

One of the most important contributions to the interior design of the coffeehouse was the introduction of the Thonet chair, the bentwood, cane-seated chair with a graceful curved back that had been previously introduced at Café Procope in Paris. Nestled under marble-topped tables, it was de rigeur for interior furnishings for many years, and remains so today in many European coffeehouses.

Designer Michael Thonet lived to see his design used all around the globe, following a series of world exhibitions of his chair. His small company, which began in about 1850, grew to the point that by 1860 he employed three hundred workers who created two hundred chairs per day. By 1896 he had exported more than 40 million chairs. One can find imitations of these chairs in Istanbul, Cairo, and all through Europe and America, but today the true Thonet chair is most likely to be found in Moravia, Bohemia, Slovakia, and in the Carpathians.

The coffeehouse was the center of learning and the exchange of ideas about current events. But not all was serious conversation; the coffeehouse was a vibrant game center where chess, *taroc*, billiards, cards, and dice were played with great enthusiasm. In Vienna's Café Central, chess tournaments were played to tremendous audiences, and those scenes have found themselves replayed many times in Austrian literature. Both the professional and the dilettante played here. A much-quoted line from the Café Central days was spoken after a messenger came to reveal that a revolution had broken out in Russia. An Austrian minister reacted dismissively, commenting, "Away with you, who is going to make a revolution in Russia? Perhaps Herr Trotsky from the Café Central?" (We now know that between 1907 and 1914 Trotsky had done more than play chess at Café Central.)

A. GRIEVE

From the early 1900s up to the late 1930s, the cabaret show was a mainstay in Austrian and German coffeehouses. Not everyone was pleased, of course, but the coffeehouse was definitely the breeding ground for both sides of each political issue that involved Germany and Austria through two world wars. One satirical cabaret followed another, appearing in both small and lavish coffeehouses. In 1934, as fascism was growing strong, there were twenty-five cabarets, each with a fiftieth chair always left empty. To fill that remaining chair would have invited the censor, who had decreed that only forty-nine seats were allowed in such cabarets. In just a few short years, the cabarets were closed and a more ominous censorship blanketed Austria.

GERMANY

To this day Germany is a serious coffee-drinking country, despite the campaign once staged by Frederick the Great to stem the flow of Deutschmarks out of the country and into the hands of those selling this "Devil's drink." His prohibition, which coincidentally also championed his own favorite beverage, beer, was engineered by German physicians who, like their French and Italian counterparts, initially disparaged the health benefits of coffee because, most likely, as one of Frederick's spokesmen said, "His Majesty was brought up on beer; many battles were fought and won by soldiers nourished on beer, and the king does not believe that coffee-drinking soldiers can be depended upon." So intense was the campaign against coffee that the government hired a special force, *Kaffee Schnufflers*, to "sniff out" illicit coffee roasters and smugglers. They failed, and even Frederick the Great had to cave in, forsaking his beloved beer.

Since the sixteenth century, social gatherings (*Kränzchen*) of the bourgeoisie involved people taking turns at playing host (wearing the requisite laurel wreath), and music, games, and cards were popular forms of entertainment for both men and women. These *Kränzchen* took place well into the nineteenth century.

During the 1700s, coffee was served in small, handleless cups called *Koppchen* (larger than the delicate Turkish cups but an obvious variation on a theme). The cups and their matching saucers were a frequent companion to card-playing aristocrats whose passion was ombre, a very popular card game in the sixteenth and seventeenth centuries.

In the nineteenth century, German *Hausfrauen* were no longer working in fields besides their husbands. Unable to accompany their mates to a coffeehouse, the women established a ritual of coffee drinking at home. *Kaffeekränzchen*, especially in Hamburg and Leipzig, were daily or sometimes weekly gatherings where ladies drank coffee and played cards with their dearest friends. Nervous husbands branded this chatter of women *Kaffeeklatsch* (coffee and gossip), but it could be seen as the first declaration of independence for German womanhood.

In the mid 1800s, dioramas of confectionery art were drawing cards for coffeehouses in Berlin, where immigrant confectioners from Austria and Switzerland were not merely bakers but sculptors. These designers created sugar or candy "pictures," particularly at Christmastime, and customers were lured into the coffeehouses featuring the most elaborate displays.

Blumchenkaffe, or "flower coffee," a term used to describe the delicate flowers painted on the inside of Dresden-quality cups, may actually be a word first used to describe the coffee itself. The watery coffee sometimes drunk in Germany offered a view of the stray grounds at the bottom of the cup. While there may be debate about the origin of *Blumchenkaffe*, the pattern in those stray grounds certainly provided work for German fortune-tellers, *Tassenfrauen*. These women became all the rage at private homes, and their "performance" of reading the coffee grounds was a uniquely formalized ritual. To keep their wits about them, they were first treated to a few cups of coffee, the best of course. Then they would fill the client's cup half full of coffee. After sipping from this cup of coffee, the "client" would hand over the cup to the *Tassenfrau* who would turn the cup over on a saucer and rotate the cup three times, to settle the grounds. Then, she would raise the cup high, peer into it with great seriousness, and read the messages—of hope and sometimes fear—in the grounds. The punsters among you can certainly see the opportunities here: "grounds for divorce," "no grounds for that," "insufficient grounds," etc.

Music Comes to the German Coffeehouse

As in every era, the coffeehouse could hardly survive on coffee sales alone. In Germany, particularly the coffeehouses of Berlin, musicales were presented by some of the most accomplished composers and musicians of the seventeenth and eighteenth centuries. This enabled the owners to charge an admission to cover the cost of the entertainment and, of course, to make a realistic profit.

Johann Sebastian Bach (1685–1750) composed his *Kaffeekantate* ("Coffee Cantata") to express sympathy with women neglected by their husbands who would squander their time at the coffeehouses. The cantata, a comical musicale with all the contemporary conflicts of family life, was also a response to aforementioned Frederick the Great's attempt to ban coffee in Germany.

Bach premiered his *Kaffeekantate*, with text by Christian Friedrich Henrici, in 1734 at Zimmermann's Caffee-Hauss, where Bach had taken over the Collegium Musicum, a philharmonic group which performed on Friday evenings from 1729 to 1740 at the coffeehouse in Leipzig.

In this silly libretto the father is distraught that his dear daughter Lizzie loves coffee so much that she'll never get married. Her reply, "Most precious of blisses, choicer than ten thousand kisses, sweeter than muscatel wine! Coffee, if my Pa would please me, only coffee will appease me, I hail thee coffee, mine!"

Her father threatens to not buy her clothes or jewelry, thinking her pigheaded about this brew, this coffee. Then he promises to find her a beau. But Lizzie declares one need not come to the house unless he would sign a marriage contract that says he will always let her brew her coffee when she craves it. Acknowledging that not only do he and his wife drink coffee, but that grandmama does too, the father finally concedes and allows his dear daughter Lizzie to drink her coffee.

No Pulitzer Prize–winning stuff, but nice fluff about an important element in the social arena of Germany in the 1700s. Considering the huge appetite the Germans have for fine coffee, it is amazing that it was ever controversial there.

Bach was not the only composer to favor coffee; Beethoven is said to have been very particular about his cup, counting off sixty beans per cup, equivalent to about two tablespoons of grounds, quite a suitable formula even today. He was the first to perform in the Prater coffeehouse, premiering his B-flat trio, and the Prater was also the scene of his last public appearance as a pianist.

No less important personages than Arnold Schoenberg and Johann Strauss, Sr., were among the German composers who visited the Prater coffeehouse either to listen or to perform, thus cementing a tradition of fine music in the Vienna coffeehouse for several generations.

ENGLAND

Coffee and Commonwealth begin
Both with one letter, both came in

Together for a Reformation,
To make's a free and sober nation.
　　　—Anonymous, "The Character of a Coffee-House
　　　by an Eye and Ear Witness, " London, 1665

William Harvey, discoverer of the principles of blood circulation, drank copious amounts of coffee, declaring it a strong benefit to one's health. "This little bean is the source of happiness and wit," he said. Not one to hog the wealth, he directed that the London College of Physicians, beneficiary of the fifty-six pounds of coffee beans he left them in his will, should brew his coffee at least once a month, for the pure pleasure of his surviving friends.

Harvey was not the first European to drink coffee nor the first to extol its virtue. The first cup of coffee brewed in England may have been drunk by Conopios, a native of Crete who served under Cyril Lucaris, the religious patriarch of Constantinople. When his boss was strangled by a henchman of the Sultan Murad IV, Conopios wisely fled to England, where he caught the interest of observers with the beverage he prepared each morning. Shortly thereafter, in 1650, the first English coffeehouse was opened in Oxford by a native of Lebanon. Called At the Angel in the Parish of St. Peter in the East, it drew hundreds of students from all corners of the British Isles, who enjoyed the drink so much that they founded the Oxford Coffee Club, forerunner to the Royal Society.

Thus began a tradition of colorful coffeehouses which served as a "window on the manners, morals and politics of the people," as Isaac Disraeli described them. London's first coffeehouse, the Pasqua Rosée, had opened in 1652 and is thought to have been part of the ushering in of the Age of Reason, that time between the English Revolution of 1688 to the French Revolution which began in 1789. This coincidence of time and place produced the perfect era for the coffeehouse, where literature, science, economics, and politics were discussed with vigor and at length by the poets and true thinkers of that age.

One sip of this will bathe drooping spirits in delight beyond the bliss of dreams.
　　　　　　　　　　　　　　　　　　—Milton

The first advertisement for coffee, now thought important enough to be housed in the British Museum, was a handbill distributed in 1651 that read: "The Vertue of the COFFEE Drink First publiquely made and sold in England, by Pasqua Rosée . . . in St. Michael's Alley in Cornhill . . . at the Signe of his own Head."

The first newspaper ad, appearing in 1657 in the *Publick Adviser* of London, made more fulsome remarks about coffee, blaring that it was the drink that ". . . closes the Orifice of the Stomack, fortifies the Heat within, helpeth Digestion, quicketh the Spirits, maketh the Heart lightsom, is good against Eye-sores, Coughs or Colds, Rhumes, Consumptions, head-ach, Dropsie, Gout, Scurvy, Kings Evil and many others."

In England, as in Italy and Austria, the introduction of coffee angered certain merchants. Those selling ale and wine felt threatened by its encroaching popularity. Britain's alehouses even launched a campaign that actually convinced Charles II to issue an order to suppress coffeehouses. But the mandate was short-lived; issued on December 29, 1675, it was retracted due to public outcry by January 8, 1676, two days before it was actually to take effect.

The London coffeehouses were unlike the rowdy taverns and had such strict codes of propriety that they were called penny universities. At that price, admission to a world of impressive thought was open to many who could not afford traditional university education at Cambridge or Oxford. Coffee cost two pennies and included newspapers and no time limit in which to finish either. By the eighteenth century, London had more than 2,000 coffeehouses, and each trade, class, and profession had its favorite.

These coffeehouses were not the elegant affairs found in Constantinople but rather dusty, simple buildings where customers' eyes smarted from the thick air of tobacco. Nor was coffee served in delicate china cups; instead it was offered in bowls or dishes.

Coffee could be had black or with spices (salt, pepper, cinnamon, cloves, spearmint), or (believe it or not) mustard. Sour cream or egg could be added to one's coffee to provide one with strength to argue one's political views. At other times an egg white was dropped into the brew during boiling to coagulate the finer grounds and pull them to the bottom of the pot. Sweeteners used were the pricey sugar or less costly molasses, and for those with more than the typical twopence for a bowl of coffee, a jigger of brandy could be poured into the brew.

English coffeehouses were such a home away from home that many men used the address of their favorite coffeehouse for their own. One could take coffee home to the missus, of course, ordering either the Turkie Berry, a roughly-ground version for less than six shillings a pound, or a pound of ground East India Berry for twenty pence, directions included, according to an ad in *Mercurius Publicus*, March 1662.

Among the old London coffeehouses are Garraway's, Lloyd's (forerunner of Lloyd's of London insurers), St. James's, Will's, White's, Slaughter's, The Grecian, Button's, Tom's, and Don Saltero's. Publishers recognized the coffeehouse as an ideal place to advertise their products, and were the first to offer papers to "lye for common chatt and entertainment in every coffee house board."

The Guardian received its mail at Button's, and the *Tatler* and *Spectator* grew out of conversations between writers Joseph Addison and Sir Richard Steele at their own favorite coffeehouse. Daniel Defoe and Henry Fielding were often seen participating in the literary conversation of the day. Samuel Johnson teamed up with actor David Garrick to form the Turk's Head, which went on to have several generations of thespians and writers as its members.

A fig for partridges and quails,
Ye dainties I know nothing of ye;
But on the highest mount in Wales,
Would choose in peace to drink my coffee.
—Jonathan Swift, 1667–1745

Coffee was so important to Dean Swift that he was quoted as saying, "The best maxim I know in life is to drink your coffee when you can, and when you cannot, to be easy without it."

Coffee made its way into British homes of the late eighteenth century as a breakfast and dinner beverage. That "other beverage," tea, had found itself a champion in the British East India Company, which argued for tea as the national beverage, not solely on its virtues but because of the revenues it brought to the company and to the British Isles.

Drinking tea and coffee became so popular that the public sought grander and more elegant places to savor these brews, and the era of the exquisite gardens, like Ranelagh and Vauxhall, began. At these monuments to English passion for flowering plants, mazes of shrubs, gracious pavilions, women could parade among the beautiful landscape like moving flora themselves, in fashionable gowns and elaborate hats and accompanied by men in morning suits and top hats. These strollers personified the elegance and leisure of the privileged class.

Although both coffee and tea were served in these gardens, the afternoon choice of the women, tea, prevailed—and tea gardens they became, ushering in a whole era of tea experiences for the English upper class.

Coffee continued to be enjoyed by British men in all stations of life, and Addison, writing in the *Tatler*, likened the coffeehouse to a men's club:

The coffee house is the place of rendezvous to all that live near it, who are thus turned to relish calm and ordinary life. It is very natural for a man who is not turned for mirthful meetings of men, or assemblies of the fair sex, to delight in that sort of conversation which we find in coffee houses. Here a man of my temper is in his element; for, if he cannot talk, he can still be more agreeable to his company, as well as pleased in himself, in being only a hearer.

Noting the penchant for political commentary among the patrons, Addison also wrote, in 1711:

I appear on Sunday nights at St. James's Coffe-House, and sometimes join the little Committee of Politicks in the Inner-Room, as one who comes there to hear and improve.

Is it any wonder that an English coffeehouse was the site for the world's first ballot box? Later it became the marriage license bureau, the post office (thus enabling those who took their mail there to at least contribute to the coffers), and the general source of information for local business.

> As long as Mocha's happy tree shall grow,
> While berries crackle, or while mills shall go;
> While smoking streams from silver sprouts shall glide,
> Or China's earth receive the sable tide,
> While coffee shall to British nymphs be dear
> While fragrant steams the bended head shall cheer
> Or grateful bitters shall delight the taste
> So long her honors, name and praise shall last.
> —Alexander Pope, 1688–1744

Pope, with "bended head," would inhale the steam from his cup of coffee in order to obtain relief from headaches. Ever quotable about his favorite drink, he also said, "Coffee!—which makes the politician wise, and see through all things with his half-shut eyes."

COFFEE-HOUSE KEEPERS' TOKENS OF THE 17TH CENTURY

UNITED STATES

I have measured out my life in coffee spoons.
—T. S. Eliot

A COFFEE MOMENT

D. K., Fort Collins, Colorado

I used to go to work on the train to Manhattan, dashing up the stairs at Grand Central Station, and heading down to Forty-fourth and Madison to the coffee shop Mecca of America, Schrafft's. I ordered the same thing every morning so often that the waitress would simply have it ready for me as I walked through the door: a steaming heavy cup of coffee and a warmed muffin with pools of butter undulating on top. The muffin was crisp on top and tender inside and made me feel good all over. All I can say about the coffee is that it wasn't black like these burnt coffees are today, it was brown. It looked like coffee and it smelled like coffee and it tasted like coffee and it always made my day. I sure miss Schrafft's.

Coffee in the United States in the mid 1600s, most particularly New York, was a beverage brewed from roasted beans and sweetened with sugar, honey, or cinnamon. By 1670 coffee had made its way to New England, and coffeehouses on the English model were in every colony. New York, Boston, and Philadelphia boasted some of the oldest and finest, and coffeehouses could also be found in Norfolk, Chicago, St. Louis, and New Orleans.

Coffeehouses did double duty: the King's Arms, the Merchants, and the Exchange in New York were often venues for criminal trials or for assembly meetings; in Boston they were host to firebrands growing tired of George II's tyranny. The most famous houses in Boston included the King's Head, the Indian Queen, and the Sun in Faneuil Hall Square. John Adams and Paul Revere plotted with their compatriots in perhaps the most significant coffeehouse at all, the Green Dragon on Union Street, which figured in nearly every social and political event in Boston for more than 135 years.

At first, coffee was roasted by neighborhood coffee merchants in small batches and delivered to customers by cart and horse. The roasting style was light, providing a sweet pure coffee flavor, and consumers ground their own beans at home with hand-cranked grinders. Following that Boston "incident," coffee was and still remains the national drink, but it has taken many turns in the way of quality and style.

As Americans moved west, coffee went with them, joining infusions made from garden herbs and sassafras root as the beverages of the trail. While Manhattan was traded for chump change and beads, the legend surrounding Fort Laramie, Wyoming, is that it was traded by Indians for tools, weapons, riding gear, and several sacks of brown-roasted Javas.

The American Army roasted green coffee beans over campfires and served it *café con leche*–style as regular rations during the Mexican War. Union soldiers during the Civil War were issued either ten pounds of green coffee beans or eight pounds of ground roasted coffee as part of their personal ration of one hundred pounds of food. The latter, a roughly dried version of coffee, was proof that instant coffee is hardly a twentieth-century invention.

A cup of coffee—real coffee—home browned, home ground, home made, that comes to you dark as a hazel eye, but changes to a golden bronze as you temper it with cream that never cheated . . . such a cup of coffee is a match for twenty blue devils and will exorcise them all.

—Henry Ward Beecher, 1813–1887

Until the 1930s and the start of World War II, coffee was a small business for most roasters. But a combination of a coffee shortage and the competition among larger companies bidding for government contracts to supply the soldiers during the war greatly influenced both the style of roasting and the quality of the beans. With increased demand, larger companies bid not on quality of the bean but on its price. Realizing that lighter roasts also meant less shrinkage of the bean, they were able to offer more "value" at lower cost along with the introduction of uniformity of taste and the convenience of preground, canned coffee.

Most of the neighborhood roasters who were so popular up to and including the 1920s were out of business by the end of World War II. The push was on for "convenience." With the introduction of electric percolators and other "easier" ways to make coffee, and less sophisticated roasting techniques, a decidedly different palate for coffee emerged.

With the rebellious sixties came the new cadre of coffee lovers and coffee entrepreneurs who had traveled extensively and sampled fine arabica coffee in Europe and the more cosmopolitan of America's big cities. They recognized the satisfaction and the lure of higher-grade coffee and gambled that better-quality beans, roasted in the European manner, would be a critical success, and they were right. Today the neighborhood roaster is back in force and delivering the goods, if not by horse and cart, certainly in upscale, lively coffee bars and coffeehouses.

Ironically, the love affair with the dark roasts is abating just at the point where regional tastes and specialty roasters have finally influenced the entire nation that the darker roasts are "better." Roasters who began in the late sixties and early seventies distinguished themselves in the then-emerging specialty coffee world by popularizing the Italian and French roasts which have always been found in San Francisco. These roasts became popular in

Seattle, which has since influenced coffee drinkers throughout the United States.

The proverbial pendulum has swung back, and in the past five years the trend has been to embrace the sweeter, more delicate taste of the light- and medium-style roasts. Many independent roasters have always roasted lighter to meet the demands of those who appreciate this style of bean, including the majority of Midwesterners and Easterners, who have steadily maintained their love for the lighter-roasted bean. Many espresso lovers have discovered that a fabulous espresso can be made with a light roast which gives a sweeter cup of exceptional intensity without a trace of the dark-roasted bitterness some people have never acquired the taste for, no matter how hard they tried.

Some roasters believe that the light roast offers the widest degree of varietal flavor. In the dark-roasting process, the natural sugars are caramelized and "cook," turning the bean darker. These sugars also change the taste and natural character of the varietals to an increased intensity of taste we now associate with French or Italian dark roasts. While light roasts will probably not kick dark roasts off the coffee merchant's shelves, they represent a taste trend for the future, one that ironically harkens back to the coffee preferences of the eighteenth century.

New Orleans

Drinking coffee in Louisiana is almost like breathing the air, a natural thing to do. The Louisiana Purchase delivered to the developing United States many coffee-loving

French towns along the Mississippi River. With the influx of the French came their recipes and love for the dark brew.

It was not just black coffee but *café au lait* that became the most popular Creole homestead drink; hot coffee and scalded milk were poured into the cup at precisely the same moment, sending an aroma of rich, bubbling brown coffee throughout the house and perhaps down into the street to greet strolling Creoles out for coffee at the local sidewalk café.

Today, as then, the standard accompaniment to coffee in Louisiana is the *beignet*, a crisp doughnut that puffs out after frying, which is served liberally covered in powdered sugar.

"*Noir comme le diable,*" a Creole would respond when asked how he liked his coffee. "*Fort comme la mort. Doux comme l'amour. Et chaud comme l'enfer.*" (Black as the devil, strong as death, sweet as love, and hot as hell.) This is a variation of the oft-quoted saying of eighteenth-century French diplomat Prince Talleyrand.

Civil War–era Cajuns considered green coffee beans to be staples. Like flour and sugar, they were packed up in 140-pound sacks, which were then stored in a cool, dark room until the woman of the house roasted them, by spreading them in a two-inch shallow pan over wood-burning ovens. Regular shakes ensured consistency of darkness. Roasted almost black, the beans were then ground by hand and brewed in a French-style drip pot, which was kept on the stove until nightfall and replenished whenever the brew ran low. The first thing a Cajun might do in the morning was put water on the stove, and the last thing at night was to take the pot off the stove. For those purists who feel that even twenty minutes is too long for a pot of coffee to sit on a warmer, the idea of Cajun-style coffee can bring shudders, but perhaps the hand-roasting, hand-grinding, and slow brewing keeps the coffee from becoming bitter.

Café noir (black coffee) remained the standard drink in New Orleans fine restaurants, beginning with Antoine's in 1840. In the century before Swiss gold mesh filters and unbleached or bleached paper filters, premier restaurants used linen filters to make their fine black coffees, washing the linen filters daily and hanging them in the rear of the restaurants to line dry. Nearly as popular as *cafée noir* was *café brûlot*, a combination of coffee, brandy, Grand Marnier, cinnamon, cloves, and orange and lemon peel, especially spectacular when its ribbon of gold-blue flame follows the alcohol down the spiraling orange peel into the bowl of dark coffee.

One unique quality of south Louisiana coffee is the addition of the ground root of chicory. Mentioned in an Egyptian papyrus in 4000 B.C., chicory was consumed in great quantities by Aristophanes, and Homer longed to refresh himself with "olives and chicory." Süleyman the Magnificent of Turkey discovered a palace guard stealing the royal coffee and mixing it with chicory (for his own enjoyment, of course). Fascinated, Süleyman ordered the guard to show him the recipe; he tried it and took credit for being the first to serve chicory with coffee in Turkey.

The first to introduce chicory in the United States was Governor James Bowdoin of Massachusetts in 1785, but the North barely followed his lead, although the South did. Nineteenth-century cookbook author Lafcadio Hearn, author of *La Cuisine Creole*, thought so highly of chicory-flavored coffee that he referred to it as "the crowning of a grand dinner . . . the pièce de résistance, the greatest *pousse-café* of all."

1950S PUBLIC HEALTH ANNOUNCEMENT

When you join others for coffee, you exchange experiences and lessen tensions. You practice skills in meeting people, firm up your ego strengths, boost your prestige, and create new cores of interest. The coffee break is the town meeting brought up to date and dressed in work clothes. It represents a lone form of democracy in the culture of bigness.

A COFFEE MOMENT

Amy Ulmer, San Marino, California

My family and I drove from Seattle to Anacortes to get on the ferry to Victoria. It was a cold day despite the fact that the calendar clearly said it was July.

At the ferry landing there was a snack bar selling cappuccino, something unusual in the days years ago before Starbucks hit Southern California, where I live. Intrigued, I ordered one, and it came in a paper cup. I sat down on the rocks to watch the ferry arrive and drink in the cappuccino and the amazing scenery all around me. It remains the best cappuccino I have ever had—just right: the flavor, the sweetness, the warmth. It was orgasmic. I think it was a combination of truly good coffee and the gorgeous surroundings. And, I must confess, the kids weren't fighting at the time, providing me with just enough peace and quiet to savor this wonderful drink.

◇◇◇

Recipes

From Espresso to Latte and Everything in Between, Including Some Great Desserts

Coffee adds a kick that really perks up the palate. Coffee gives a wonderful flavor to barbecue sauces and gravies, makes a terrific glaze for ham, and is the perfect addition to bean dishes like chili or Boston baked beans. Try it over brisket instead of onion soup, or add it to your favorite beef or lamb stew recipe instead of red wine, stock, or water. Coffee makes a fabulous marinade because its natural acidity tenderizes even the most humble cut of meat and adds a richness and heartiness without additional fat or calories. Try adding coffee to some of your own classic dishes, or try some of these at your next dinner party. Those recipes with an asterisk after the title were contributed by my friend Gary Stotsky, an expert and enthusiastic baker. Many thanks!

CLASSIC BARBECUE SAUCE WITH COFFEE

The addition of coffee in this sauce adds a richness that is both subtle and a good balance for the spices.

- $1/2$ cup coffee
- $1^1/2$ cups ketchup
- 1 onion
- $1/2$ cup melted margarine
- 6 tablespoons lemon juice
- 2 tablespoons prepared mustard
- 6 tablespoons brown sugar
- 2 tablespoons Worcestershire sauce
- 4 tablespoons prepared horseradish

Combine all ingredients in a food processor or blender and purée. Brush on grilled meats or chicken. Can keep in the refrigerator for several weeks.

About 3 cups

MOLE SAUCE*

This is a perfect sauce for serving over poached turkey or chicken breast slices; wonderful for après Thanksgiving when you think you can't eat another piece of turkey.

- 1 large poblano chili pepper
- 3 tablespoons olive oil
- 2 garlic cloves, chopped
- 1 cup onion, chopped
- $1/2$ cup celery, finely chopped
- $1/2$ teaspoon cayenne pepper
- $1/2$ teaspoon ground cardamom
- $1/8$ teaspoon or pinch of ground cloves

$^1/_2$ cup cold coffee
1 ounce unsweetened chocolate, finely chopped
1 $^1/_2$ cups chicken broth
Chopped almonds for garnish, as desired

Wash and dry chili pepper and char it over a flame until skin is blackened all over. Let pepper cool in a paper bag, then slice away the charred skin and remove the seeds from inside the pepper. Chop remaining skin finely and set aside.

Heat olive oil in a saucepan over medium heat and add the garlic and onion and sauté until the onion is golden brown, approximately 10 minutes. Add the celery and continue to sautè a few more minutes. Add the spices and the reserved chopped chili to the pan and stir to combine. Add the coffee and raise the heat, stirring constantly, until the liquid has evaporated. Add the chocolate and stir well. Add chicken broth and bring the mixture to a boil, stirring frequently.

Lower the heat to a simmer and simmer the mixture uncovered for 20 minutes. Purée the sauce in a food processor or blender. Serve over chicken or turkey, garnished with chopped almonds.

About 2 cups

BEEF STEW

4 tablespoons virgin olive oil
2 $^1/_2$ pounds stew meat, cut into chunks
1 clove garlic, crushed
2 large onions, sliced
4 tablespoons flour
1 cup water
1 cup strong freshly brewed coffee

$1/4$ teaspoon each oregano and marjoram
$1/2$ teaspoon pepper
1 teaspoon salt
1 cup baby carrots
2 large white potatoes, peeled cut into chunks

Heat oil in a deep frying pan and when hot, gently put in the meat. Brown on all sides. Add garlic and onions and cook until soft. Remove from pan and add flour to remaining oil in pan. Add seasonings, water, and coffee and stir until slightly thickened. Return meat, onions, and garlic. Cover and bring to a boil, then simmer about 45 minutes. At this point add the carrots and potatoes and additional water as necessary, and simmer another 30 minutes. Serve over rice or buttered noodles.

6 ample servings

COFFEE ORANGE WHIPPED YAMS

$1/4$ cup raisins, for garnish
4 tablespoons strong freshly brewed coffee
4 large yams, baked
4 tablespoons fresh orange juice
Dash each of ground cinnamon and cardamom
$1/4$ cup butter

Soak raisins in just-brewed coffee, strain, and remove. Whip all other ingredients thoroughly; adjust seasonings to taste and serve hot. Can be served in scooped-out orange halves or carved-out small pumpkin gourds. Garnish with coffee-soaked raisins.

4 servings

SWEETS FOR BREAKFAST, COFFEE BREAK, AND DESSERTS AFTER DINNER

BEIGNETS

There are as many ways to make beignets as there are people in New Orleans to enjoy them, but this classic recipe remains the best I have ever tried.

> 1 cup whole milk
> 1 tablespoon shortening; Crisco is fine although old-timers used lard (go ahead, I won't say a word and I can assure you they will definitely taste lighter and more delicate)
> 2 tablespoons sugar
> 1 package dry yeast (two teaspoons)
> 3 cups all-purpose white flour
> 1 teaspoon nutmeg
> 1 teaspoon salt
> 1 egg
> Confectioners' sugar for dusting

Stirring constantly, heat the milk over a low flame just to the scalding point. In a bowl, mix shortening and sugar and slowly add the hot milk, stirring until the sugar is dissolved and the shortening is melted. Cool mixture to lukewarm, then add the yeast and stir until it has completely dissolved.

In another bowl, sift the flour with the nutmeg and salt and gradually add about half of the dry mixture to the milk mixture to form a batter. When the batter is smooth, add the egg and beat it in until very well blended. Then add the remaining flour mixture to the batter and stir again until the entire batter batch is smooth. Cover the bowl with a towel and set aside to rise to double in size; this will take an hour.

Place dough on a floured board and knead gently and roll out to a thickness of one-quarter inch. Cut the dough into diamond shapes with a sharp knife and cover these with a towel and set aside for 45 minutes.

Heat a mild-flavored oil, like safflower oil, to 385 degrees; check the temperature with a thermometer. Fry the beignets, turning only once. When golden brown, lift out gently, drain them on a paper towel, and dust liberally with confectioners' sugar. Serve with chicory-laced coffee, listen to Dixieland jazz, and enjoy!

About 2 dozen

CAFE SCONES L'ORANGE

As a beverage, instant coffee lacks the decided punch we have all come to know and love about our favorite drink in its freshly brewed form. But, instant coffee is wonderfully convenient for cooking and baking, because it dissolves so easily and blends so well. These are sinfully rich tasting and satisfying enough for breakfast.

2 $\frac{1}{4}$ cups all purpose flour
$\frac{1}{2}$ teaspoon salt
2 tablespoons sugar
1 orange rind, grated or zested
4 tablespoons sweet butter (unsalted)
2 tablespoons instant coffee
$\frac{1}{2}$ pint (approx.) buttermilk
12 sugar cubes
$\frac{1}{4}$ pint orange juice

Mix together the flour, salt, and sugar and add the orange rind. Rub in the butter until mixture resembles cornmeal. Dissolve instant coffee in the buttermilk and pour slowly into the dry mixture, binding the dough. Roll out dough onto a floured surface in a circle and cut into pie slices. Place on a greased and floured pan. Dip sugar cubes in the orange juice and press one in the center of each scone. Bake in 475-degree oven for 10 to 15 minutes or until browned. Cool slightly, but serve warm. Perfect with coffee whipped cream or orange marmalade.

About 1 dozen

Café Brûlée

I love crème brûlée, especially with a great cup of coffee. This recipe takes an ambrosial dessert to new heights.

> **3 cups heavy cream**
> **6 egg yolks**
> **1 tablespoon sugar**
> **1 1/2 teaspoons real vanilla**
> **4 tablespoons instant powdered coffee**
> **2 tablespoons coffee liqueur, like Tia Maria or Kahlúa**
> **2 tablespoons coarse brown sugar**

In a double boiler or pan of simmering water, place a bowl with the cream in it.

Using a separate bowl, beat the egg yolks and slowly add the sugar and vanilla, the coffee and coffee liqueur, and gently stir this mixture into the warmed cream. Continue to cook, stirring constantly, until the sauce is thick enough to coat the back of a wooden spoon.

Using a fine sieve, strain the cream into individual ramekins. Put these into a large shallow dish that is filled with hot water (up to the rim of the ramekins). Carefully place in the oven and bake at 300 degrees for about 35 to 45 minutes, or until the middle of the custard is firm. Remove the custard dishes from the pan, cool, cover and then chill. Sift the brown sugar atop the chilled custard and place in a preheated broiler as close to the heat as possible and broil until the sugar caramelizes. Having a glass door to the oven helps! Remove, cool, and chill again for two to three hours.

4 servings

COFFEE CHOCOLATE CAKE*

1 box of chocolate cake mix
$^1/_2$ cup oil
1 small package of chocolate instant pudding (3 ounces)
4 eggs
$^3/_4$ cup strongly brewed coffee
$^3/_4$ cup coffee liqueur

Mix all the ingredients together well and pour into a greased and floured 9-inch-by-13-inch cake pan. Bake at 350 degrees for 45 minutes, or until a cake tester comes clean. Let cool and then add the following icing:

KAHLÚA ICING*

$^1/_2$ pint whipping cream
2 tablespoons sugar
1 tablespoon Kahlúa
1 teaspoon vanilla

Whip cream with sugar and add flavorings until thoroughly mixed. Spread evenly on cooled cake.

Makes 1 cup

CHOCOLATE-FLAVORED COFFEE CAKE

$\frac{1}{2}$ cup butter (one stick)
1 cup Hawaiian washed raw sugar
3 large eggs
$1\frac{1}{2}$ tablespoons pure vanilla
$\frac{1}{8}$ teaspoon pure almond extract
2 cups unbleached cake flour
$\frac{1}{2}$ teaspoon salt
2 teaspoons ground cinnamon
1 teaspoon baking powder
$\frac{1}{4}$ teaspoon baking soda
$\frac{1}{4}$ cup buttermilk
2 tablespoons instant coffee, granulated,
  not powdered
4 ounces semisweet chocolate
$\frac{3}{4}$ cup water

Butter and flour two round eight-inch cake pans and set aside. Cream the butter and sugar together and then beat in eggs, one at a time. Slowly add the vanilla and almond extract. Blend well. Sift dry ingredients together. Add buttermilk and the butter mixture, alternating each one until all are mixed in gently into the dry ingredients. Set aside. Combine chocolate, water, and coffee in a small saucepan, and cook gently over low heat until chocolate and coffee are fully dissolved. Add this liquid mixture to batter and mix thoroughly. Pour batter into the floured pans and bake at 350 degrees until firm, about 45 minutes. Cool before icing with the following:

MOCHA COFFEE ICING

$1/2$ cup strong brewed coffee
6 ounces semisweet chocolate
1 teaspoon pure vanilla
$1/2$ stick butter

In a saucepan, place the chocolate, coffee, and vanilla and cook on medium to low heat, stirring frequently. When the chocolate mixture is thoroughly melted, pour into a bowl and beat in the butter.

About 3/4 cup

COFFEE CHIFFON PIE*

Graham cracker pie crust (purchase in bakery section of grocery store or make your own)
1 tablespoon unflavored gelatin
4 eggs, separated
$1/2$ teaspoon salt
1 cup sugar
1 tablespoon lemon juice
$1/2$ cup strongly brewed coffee (hot)
$3/4$ cup strongly brewed coffee (cold)

Soften the gelatin in the cold coffee for five minutes. Beat egg yolks and add 1/2 cup of the sugar, the salt and the hot coffee and cook in a double boiler until thick, like a custard. Add the gelatin mixture and the lemon juice. Cool slightly.

Beat the four egg whites with the remaining sugar until stiff. Then fold the stiffly beaten egg whites into the coffee-custard mixture. Put the newly mixed custard into a pie pan lined with a graham cracker crust and chill overnight. Served chilled with whipped cream.

C OFFEE M OCHA M OUSSE

2 cups chocolate chips (or small broken pieces of semisweet
   chocolate)
$^1/_2$ cup sugar
3 whole eggs
4 tablespoons coffee liqueur (or Vanilla Coffee Liqueur, page 123)
1 cup boiling milk

Boil the milk. In the order listed above, place the ingredients in a blender and purée for about 30 seconds. (The boiling milk will "cook" the eggs). Pour the liquid mixture into eight demitasse cups and cover tightly. Chill in the refrigerator until ready to serve, at least one hour. Top with real whipped cream and dust with instant coffee granules.

8 servings

C OFFEE D ATE C AKE

$^3/_4$ cup unsalted butter
2 teaspoons instant coffee
1 cup brown sugar
$^1/_2$ cup dates, cut up
$^1/_2$ cup whole pecans
$^1/_2$ cup white sugar
2 eggs

1 cup cake flour sifted with a pinch of salt and 1 ¹/₂ teaspoon baking powder
¹/₃ cup whole milk
¹/₂ teaspoon pure vanilla

Melt 1/2 cup (one stick) butter with the brown sugar and instant coffee; when dissolved, pour into an eight-inch square pan. Sprinkle the dates all around, then place the pecans in an elegant pattern, rounded side down.

In a bowl, cream together the remaining 1/4 cup butter with the white sugar and blend in the eggs. Add sifted dried ingredients alternately with the milk, and mix thoroughly. Add vanilla. Pour batter gently over the pecan and date glaze and bake for 40 to 45 minutes in a 350-degree oven. Remove pan and invert immediately onto a platter, but let the cake rest about 5 minutes before lifting the pan off. Serve with coffee whipped cream (below).

Coffee Whipped Cream

This is wonderful atop Irish coffee or on any coffee-flavored cake or pie recipe. Or just plop a huge tablespoon on a plain cup of joe—wow!

¹/₂ cup heavy cream (chilled)
6 teaspoons sugar
3 teaspoons instant coffee

Whip the chilled heavy cream with the sugar and instant coffee. Chill at least three hours. Rewhip until peaks form. Serve immediately.

Makes 1 ¹/₄ cups

BISCOTTI

These twice-baked Italian cookies (a very close relative of the mandelbrot of German and Russian baking) are intended for dipping. The choices now are fabulous, from white and dark chocolate covered, to cranberry walnut. I love the scent and the taste of anise (the spice of licorice) in these, and they're medium hard for dipping.

- 2$^{1}/_{4}$ cups all-purpose flour
- $^{1}/_{2}$ cup unsweetened cocoa
- $^{1}/_{2}$ cup finely ground, lightly toasted almonds
- 1$^{3}/_{4}$ teaspoons baking powder
- $^{1}/_{4}$ teaspoon ground aniseed or pulverize two star anise
- $^{1}/_{2}$ cup unsalted butter, at room temperature
- $^{2}/_{3}$ cup brown sugar
- 2 large eggs
- 2 teaspoons instant coffee dissolved in 1 tablespoon of freshly brewed hot coffee
- 6 ounces semisweet chocolate, melted

Combine the flour, cocoa, almonds, baking powder, and aniseed and set aside. In another bowl, cream butter until light, and then add the sugar and continue to beat until the mixture is light and creamy. Add the two eggs, one at a time, and beat until smooth. Stir in the coffee and then add the dry ingredients. Mix until completely combined.

Turn the dough onto a floured surface and divide into two parts. Roll each part of the dough until it's about 12 inches long, and transfer to a greased and powdered baking sheet. Do not have them touch, as they will expand because of the baking powder. Bake about 20 minutes in a preheated 350-degree oven. Remove and allow to cook on the baking sheet for another 15 minutes.

Using a knife with a serrated blade, cut each piece on the diagonal into 3/4-inch slices. Put the cut sides down and bake again for about 8 minutes, or until the edges look "toasted." Transfer to a wire rack to cool.

To dip, melt the chocolate in a double boiler and then dip one end only into the chocolate, allowing the excess to drip back into the melted chocolate. Place the biscotti on a piece of waxed paper until the chocolate sets. Can be stored in an airtight container.

About 2 dozen

COFFEE ALMOND CHOCOLATE CHIP COOKIES

These are a snap to make, but better make the complete recipe, as they'll be gone in a flash. A great diversion from the typical biscotti cookie.

- ³/₄ cup brown sugar, packed
- 1 cup unsalted butter
- 2 cups unbleached white flour
- 2 teaspoons pure almond extract
- 4 teaspoons instant coffee
- 8 ounces semisweet chocolate chips
- 1 cup chopped roasted, unsalted almonds

Cream together the sugar and butter. Add flour, almond extract, and coffee. Gingerly mix in almonds and chocolates (hands are best!). Bake in an oven at 350 degrees for 10 minutes only, or until slightly brown.

About 2 dozen

COFFEE AND FRUIT PRESERVE

This is a rich version of a dried fruit compote that has an added kick with coffee. To gild the lily, add coffee whipped cream (page 110). This is good warm or cool.

- 1 cup pitted and chopped dried prunes
- 1 cup dried and chopped apricots
- 1/3 cup strong black brewed coffee
- 1/3 cup fresh orange juice mixed with 2 1/2 teaspoon grated orange rind
- 1/2 teaspoon cinnamon
- 1/2 teaspoon cardamom
- 1 cup medium-ground walnuts

Combine everything but the walnuts together into a small heavy saucepan and simmer about 5 to 10 minutes over a moderate heat. Blend in the walnuts. Excellent warm or chilled. Makes a nice condiment with pork or turkey, too.

About 2⅔ cups

COFFEE TRUFFLES

Coffee and chocolate are naturals for each other, both in the brew and in sweets. We particularly like this Hungarian-style truffle which has long been a specialty of a dear family friend, who graciously gave me this recipe, although she begged anonymity. She gave friends, family, and other loved ones this pleasurable treat every holiday season. "It's time for the next generation to carry on the tradition," she said.

- 1/3 cup freshly brewed espresso
- 7/8 cup of fine granulated sugar
- 1 cup ground almonds

2 tablespoons finely ground coffee, e.g., Turkish or Arab coffee
$^1/_4$ teaspoon almond extract (or to taste)

Combine about 3/4 cup of the sugar with the espresso in a small saucepan and simmer over a medium flame, stirring occasionally, until the liquid becomes very syrupy; this should take about 10 minutes. Add the nuts and stir gently, then remove the pan from the heat. Refrigerate overnight.

Mix about 2 tablespoons of sugar with the ground coffee. Take the cooled sugar-espresso-almond mixture and drip about 1/8 to 1/4 teaspoon of almond extract into the "dough" and mix gently. Tear off a good pinch of dough and then make little balls, about 1/2 inch in diameter, and roll each ball in the ground-coffee–sugar mixture until well coated. Place them on a platter that has been covered with waxed paper; cover the balls with another sheet of waxed paper and refrigerate. Serve with a demitasse of espresso.

Truffle skirts, like tiny cupcake holders, are available in fine kitchenware shops and add a nice finished touch to these scrumptious candies. To package in gift tins, layer between waxed paper. Refrigerate until ready to give or serve.

About 1 dozen truffles

Rum and Coffee Sauce

Serve hot over plain crepes, vanilla ice cream, or plain angel food cake.

1 cup brown sugar
$1^1/_2$ cups hot, strong black brewed coffee
2 tablespoons arrowroot
3 tablespoons cold black brewed coffee
3 tablespoons butter
3 tablespoons dark rum

Melt the sugar in a heavy skillet over moderate heat, stirring often until it is melted and a pale brown color. *Slowly* add the hot coffee (to prevent splattering). Blend together the arrowroot and the cold coffee and pour into the heated sauce, stirring until it is thickened and just barely boiling. Remove from heat and blend in the butter and dark rum, mixing thoroughly.

Makes 2 cups

CLASSIC COFFEE DRINKS

A Word About Espresso

The ultimate coffee drink is an espresso *ristretto* of full, rich flavor from beans that have been immediately ground and quickly brewed. The word *espresso* is Italian, of course, but comes from the French word that originally meant "expressly for you." In today's variation of the word, most likely derived from the quickness with which people down their *espresso* at stand-up bars, *espresso* has come to mean "made on the spur of the moment." In other variations of the word, *espresso* means "made fresh," and neither thoughtlessly nor impulsively.

Espresso is *poco ma buono*, small but good, and this is especially true of espresso *ristretto*, with its sparse use of water and shorter extraction time. Espresso *ristretto* uses seven grams of coffee with only one ounce or less of water, with an extraction time of only twenty-five to thirty-five seconds. The grind should be adjusted to be slightly finer so that the slowed extraction can be accomplished by tamping or pressing the coffee with extra pressure. This gives an intensely rich espresso flavor.

Other versions of "true espresso" call for one and one-half ounces, filling the cup only halfway. Each serving is made with two tablespoons of ground espresso beans and, when perfectly brewed (extraction requires about thirty seconds), should have a layer of foam on the top. Although this small quantity may look lost in the three-ounce demitasse cup, it is a concentrate of perfect flavor. Drink it *solo* as the Italians do, in one quick gulp to enjoy its fresh full taste.

The larger cup of weaker coffee (that is, the nonespresso type) is referred to as *lungo*, "to pull long," to yield a larger serving. You can use three to four ounces of water through espresso grounds with an extraction time of twenty to twenty-five seconds. Though it uses the same amount of coffee (two tablespoons), *lungo* uses more water and provides about a three-ounce serving of espresso. A *doppio*, which in Italian is a double espresso, uses twice the measure of ground coffee and water to produce a three-ounce serving, actually two servings in one.

Variations include *con panna*, with whipped cream; *Americano*, with milk and/or sugar in a full six-ounce cup; *breve*, a single shot of espresso with heated half-and-half; *Cubano*, a *doppio* brewed with raw sugar. *Granita* is espresso that has been frozen and crushed and is served like ice cream in a cup with a spoon, and iced espresso consists of a cooled single shot of espresso sweetened with sugar in a six-ounce glass with ice.

Milk that is added to espresso drinks is said to "mark" the brew. Because the Italian word for "marked" is *macchiato*, an espresso with a mark of frothed milk is espresso *macchiato*, while *latte macchiato* is the opposite of espresso *macchiato*, it is steamed milk "marked" with a spot of espresso. (The word *spot* is often used interchangeably with the word *mark*.)

If you have a Moka or espresso machine, you should use about one and one-half tablespoons of fine ground coffee; a single shot of espresso should provide about one and one-quarter ounces of liquid in about twenty seconds; a double shot would be two ounces, but in the same time with twice as much ground coffee (about three tablespoons).

Steamed milk is a big part of espresso drinks, and there is a difference, albeit slight, between steamed milk and foamed milk. The temperature is 150–170 degrees Fahrenheit for steamed milk and about 5 degrees less for foamed milk, a result of the extra air incorporated into the milk.

FOAMED AND STEAMED MILK

Start with cold milk in a clean stainless steel pitcher that can help you feel the milk's temperature. Because milk will increase in volume following this process, fill the steamer with one-third milk for foaming and two-thirds full for steaming.

To assure that there is no residual condensed water in the line, open up the steam valve for a second or two.

Then put the steel pitcher under the steam jet with the tip barely under the surface of the milk.

Open the steam valve slowly yet fully, making sure to keep the tip of the steam jet barely under the surface.

Finally, lower the pitcher and add more air as you foam.

WITHOUT FOAM

To warm milk without foaming, place the nozzle of the steam jet close to the bottom of the pitcher and heat until the pitcher becomes too hot to handle.

Turn off the valve before removing the pitcher or the pressure from the open jet will splatter hot milk and possibly burn you.

Open the valve for a couple of seconds to clear out any milk that may remain, a good preventative maintenance step.

Wipe the steam jet clear with a damp cloth, dry, and put aside.

THE BEAN AND THE GRIND

Espresso is not just a brewing method, but a blend of beans, a name of a beverage and the color of a dark roast, often referred to as Italian or French dark roast, although there really is no industry standard for the exact color of the dark roast.

Caffe espresso, the beverage, is the pure essence of the bean, made with gravity with water under pressure. Tamping is the amount of pressure on the grounds packed into a filter. If the grounds are packed firmly, the water will flow through slowly, an exceptional way to obtain the fullest extraction of flavor. The pour should be not unlike thick syrup or honey dripping from a spoon.

The ideal grind is a cone filter grind or an extra fine grind with some granules of coffee beans showing. A powdery grind can be best achieved from a burr-type grinder.

Most coffee merchants use Ethiopia Yergacheffe, dark Sumatrans and other Indonesians, Guatemala Antiguas and other exceptional Central American beans roasted dark for their espresso blends; in Italy they use quite a lot of Brazilian coffee.

As described earlier, softened water is critical for use with espresso machines to make sure the grinds do not clog the machine. If your city does not have soft water (150–200 TDS, or total dissolved solids), use a commercial filter system like a Brita.

CAPPUCCINO

The word cappuccino is Italian (but of course!) and comes from the resemblance of the drink to the unique brown hooded robe worn by Capuchin friars, a Roman Catholic order. It is the hood or "cap" of this robe that has come to describe the foam on the top of a properly made cappuccino. Unlike most coffee and milk drinks, cappuccino has both foamed and steamed milk added in increments of one-third each to one-third of espresso coffee.

- 2 ounces espresso
- 2 ounces steamed milk
- 2 ounces frothed milk

For each serving, brew the espresso, preferably with softened water so that it doesn't clog the espresso machine. Then pour the steamed milk onto the bottom third of the cup. Pour the espresso slowly into the steamed milk and then carefully spoon the frothed or foamed milk on top to fill the cup. It is important to follow this layered order so that the espresso settles between the milk and the foam. The frothed milk should be about 140 to 160 degrees Fahrenheit. Timing is essential here, so always prepare the frothed milk *before* brewing the espresso.

Variation: espresso and milk only with about one and one-half ounces of espresso to two ounces of foam.

Variation: to each two-thirds cup strong espresso coffee add one-third cup hot milk and sweeten to taste. Pour into cups and dust with cinnamon, powdered cocoa, or nutmeg. Serve in tall thin cups.

CAFFÈ LATTE

In Italy, this is the same steamed milk and coffee drink as the French café au lait, but a much smaller serving. Some Italian latte lovers make it with hazelnut, almond, or other nut flavorings or other syrups.

1 shot of espresso
6 to 8 ounces whole milk

In separate pots, prepare coffee and scald milk. Pour hot steamed milk onto the espresso and serve. Makes one traditional cup or two demitasse cups.

Café Noir

This is a hot black drink, not unlike espresso, served with sugar cubes which one dips halfway into the coffee so that the soaked sugar cubes are pristine white on the top and brown on the bottom, not unlike ducks swimming on a pond or lake. These sugar cubes, called *canard* (duck) in France, are special treats for French children, who often linger at the table of adults in hopes of those treats.

The Swiss take the concept of little ducks a step further with a coffee ceremony known as *canardli*. A special little glass or silver dish, shaped like a duck, is used to hold the Swiss cherry liqueur, kirsch, which is poured into a little depression that is in the dish. With a small silver spoon, you dip a sugar cube into the kirsch and pop it in your mouth or hold it between your teeth as you sip black coffee.

The tradition of drinking hot beverages with a sugar cube in your mouth is popular in many countries with coffee and tea, particularly Russia.

CAFÉ CON LECHE

The Spanish version of *café au lait*, this drink consists of dark roast coffee (brewed by the drip method), mixed with sugar to taste and served with heated rather than scalded milk. Warm buttered bread is a common accompaniment.

The Cuban version is a totally different taste sensation and is available everywhere in Florida, but particularly in Miami, where thousands of Cubans have migrated from their homeland. Cuban coffee comes in a variety of strengths and roasting intensities, but one stellar one is Tilom. The *café con leche* made with Tilom uses very strong, very densely ground espresso and at least five teaspoons of sugar, nearly one-quarter cup, which is placed underneath the grounds so that the water pours through the grounds and through the sugar, dissolving it along the way. Then very hot milk is added to made a very strong, very sweet, very Cuban delight, *café con leche*.

Like many coffee-drinking cultures, the Cubans drink it all day long, and many businesses pass out demitasse-sized plastic cups with a strong espresso which people drink like a shot.

The Cuban version of biscotti is a light "toast" much like a fat yet airy breadstick, which is cut in half and slathered with butter to be eaten along with one's *café* or dunked directly into the cup.

Turkish Coffee

Below is a recipe for *mahout*, or medium-sweet Arabic or Turkish coffee; adding more sugar would be a *helou* or *sukkar ziada* recipe; unsweetened would be *murra*. Even if you enjoy your coffee black, the first time you try Turkish coffee, you should add sugar; otherwise it will taste so bitter you probably won't enjoy it.

Modern Recipe for Turkish Coffee

2 tablespoons roasted finely ground coffee
1 heaping teaspoon sugar
3 small coffee cups of water
Pinch of ground cardamom

Combine ingredients in a saucepan or an *ibrik* and stir well. Bring to a boil and, as a froth (*wesh*) appears on top, remove the pot from the stove and stir.

Return to the heat until the froth rises a second time. Boil briefly, then set aside for a few seconds.

Raising the pot, carefully pour a nice head of froth onto each cup, then pour in the rest of the sugar and coffee mixture. Grounds will settle in a minute or two. This recipe makes about three Turkish cupsful.

Variation: Boil three ounces of water with two heaping teaspoons of sugar; add one heaping teaspoon of powdered or very finely ground coffee and boil up to three times before removing from the fire. Add a little cold water. Serve the froth first, then carefully pour or spoon the thick brew into two cups.

Variation: One heaping teaspoon powdered coffee with one heaping teaspoon sugar for one small Turkish cup of water. Put all ingredients in the *tanaka* and boil. When froth rises, remove from the heat, stir and then return to the heat until the froth rises again. Flavor with orange blossom water or cardamom seeds at this point. Remove, tapping the pot a few times to help the grounds settle. If you have difficulty getting out the froth, shake the pot slightly.

ARABIAN COFFEE

6 cardamom pods
¼ cup cold water
1 heaping tablespoon dark roast coffee, coarsely ground

Pound the cardamom pods gently in a very clean mortar and pestle. Put pods, water, and coffee in an *ibrik* or very small saucepan and bring to a boil. Simmer over a very low heat for about 15 minutes, or until the coffee grounds settle. Serve *qahwa* in traditional tiny Arab coffee cups, which hold about two tablespoons of coffee each. It is bitter and not to everyone's taste, and never served with sugar. This makes two cups of coffee that is definitely the "real thing."

CAFÉ AU LAIT

In France, breakfast is frequently a large bowl of café au lait, *rather than a cup, the better to warm one's hands in the cool of the morning or to dip in a brioche or croissant.*

1 ½ cups strong hot coffee, preferably brewed using a drip method
1 ½ cups whole milk

In separate pots, prepare coffee and scald milk (no nonfat here!). Pour hot milk and hot coffee simultaneously into each cup. Serves two.

COFFEE WITH CALVADOS

The Normandy liqueur, calvados, is a strong distilled apple cider that is sweet and tart at the same time and a popular addition to coffee. It is not uncommon on cold Parisian mornings for workers to order this drink, made with one-half calvados and one-half strong black coffee. Perhaps this is the origin of the old French saying "A cup of coffee for an old man is like a doorpost, for it supports and strengthens him."

CAFÉ BRÛLOT
(CAFÉ AU DIABLE)

A dramatic after-dinner coffee drink, *café brûlot* is best done in the kitchen if you're inexperienced. After a few practice sessions, you could bring a chafing dish to the table and wow your guests no end.

Café au diable is made with both lemon and orange and granulated sugar; *café brûlot* is made with sugar cubes, although the classic recipe from Antoine's Restaurant in New Orleans does not use sugar cubes but adds, instead, Grand Marnier along with the brandy (which is always French, but of course). Antoine's also peels an orange in a one-piece spiral and studs the peel with cloves for an added dash. The other ingredients for both recipes are the same.

24 cubes of sugar
6 whole cloves (or more, to taste)
3/4 cup cognac or brandy
2 cinnamon sticks, broken
Grated rind of one small lemon
Grated rind of one small orange
3 cups hot, strong coffee, made with chicory

In a chafing dish or shallow pan, place all the ingredients except the coffee and heat over medium heat, stirring gently. When fully heated, ignite and flame the brandy. When the flame burns out, slowly pour in coffee and blend by lifting some of the mixture with a ladle and pouring it back into the chafing dish. When thoroughly mixed, ladle into eight demitasse cups.

VANILLA COFFEE LIQUEUR

This is a great hostess gift or holiday gift for all of your coffee-loving friends. It's excellent over ice cream, as an after-dinner drink alone or in coffee, or in any way you would use a flavored liqueur.

1 1/2 cups granulated brown sugar
1 cup granulated sugar
2 cups water
1/2 cup instant coffee powder
3 cups vodka
1 whole vanilla bean, split

Combine the sugars with the water and bring to a boil. Boil for about five minutes, then gradually stir in the instant coffee and heat until the coffee is dissolved. Remove from heat and cool. Add the vodka and vanilla bean and mix thoroughly. Pour into a decanter-style bottle or into slim bottles suitable for gift-giving. Cover all containers tightly and let rest for at least two weeks before drinking.

STRANGE BREW (POOR PERSON'S CAPPUCCINO)

Wearable-art designer Karen Strange swears this is not only a great way to start the day, it's perfect for those who don't have a milk steamer.

$^1/_2$ **cup espresso coffee**
$^1/_2$ **cup nonfat milk**

Brew the coffee to desired strength. In the meantime, put the milk in the microwave and heat for one minute. Pour the two concoctions together at the same time in a hand-warming bowl and dunk in your favorite croissant or toast. Serves one indulgent yet happy person.

VANILLA-CINNAMON COFFEE

This is one of the simplest and most delicious flavored coffees I know of, and it's perfect for a small group. You can certainly substitute ground cardamom for the cinnamon to obtain an equally enjoyable brew.

$^1/_2$ **teaspoon ground cinnamon**
2-inch piece of vanilla bean
12 cups strong coffee

Put the ground cinnamon and the vanilla bean on top of the grounds *before* brewing. Brew as normal. Remove bean and pour.

SUNDAY MORNING COFFEE

This eclectic recipe combines the smoothness of a Mexican coffee liqueur with the punch of tequila. Best to drink this only if planning to stay in bed to read the entire Sunday edition of the New York Times.

> $^1/_2$ **pint whipping cream**
>   **8 cups fresh, hot coffee**
>   **2 teaspoons sugar**
>   **1 teaspoon fresh orange juice**
>   **8 ounces Mexican coffee liqueur (e.g., Tia Maria, Kahlúa, or the Vanilla-Coffee Liqueur above)**
>   **4 ounces tequila**
>   **1 ounce unsweetened chocolate, shaved**

Whip cream in a small bowl until soft peaks form. Stir in sugar and orange juice and refrigerate. To serve, brew coffee fresh. Place one ounce of coffee liqueur and one-half ounce of tequila in each of eight cups. Fill with hot coffee. Drop a dollop of whipped cream on each and sprinkle with shaved chocolate.

IRISH COFFEE

>   **Hot, strong coffee**
>   **1 jigger of Irish whiskey per serving**
>   **Whipped cream**
>   **1 teaspoon sugar per serving**

Pour coffee into "Irish coffee glasses" or wineglasses, add sugar and whiskey, and top with whipped cream.

Variation: Add Benedictine or Kahlúa. It won't be Irish, but you'll be too mellow to care.

ABOUT THOSE OTHER COFFEES . . .

Iced Coffees

Water ices, frappes, and iced coffee drinks are refreshing, soothing, and thirst quenching. The lack of refrigeration for millennia apparently stopped no one who wanted to have a cool drink on a hot day. The Arabic word for cold drink is *sharbat*, the root word for "sorbet" or "sherbet." Sherbets, or water ices, have been around a long time, originating in the third century B.C. in China, traveling to the Middle East and then through Renaissance Italy and, finally, to the "new" world.

The original iced coffee, *mazagran*, mostly likely was named after the Algerian fortress where the drink was popularized by the French colonial troops occupying the North African deserts. This original recipe is made from coffee syrup and cold water. Concentrated coffee syrup keeps for several months, an ideal recipe for any long, hot summer.

One pound of ground coffee and three and one-half pints of water will make a strong enough brew for a coffee syrup. It is critical to strain it well, even up to three times, to make sure there are no remaining grounds. Add three pounds of sugar, stir and bring to a boil, then cool. Pour the heavy syrup into sterilized glass bottles and store in a cool place and use as desired: over ice, over ice cream, with crushed ice, topped with whipped cream, and so on.

Iced coffee uses freshly brewed coffee that is brewed double strength then cooled, but the coffee should only be made at most three hours in advance. Some common flavorings are lemon peel, fresh mint, Angostura bitters, rum, chocolate, honey, coconut and vanilla- and coffee-flavored ice creams. Although milk is a favorite for hot coffee drinks, cream works better in cold coffee drinks because it has a more intense flavor. Use coffee concentrate or frozen orange juice in ice cubes to add sparkle and taste without further diluting the coffee.

As international as hot coffee, iced coffee drinks fall under such names as *refrescos de café*, *cafés glaces*, frappes, frosts, froths, floats, nectars, and even milk shakes. Mixed with cream, it is *café Liegeois*.

GRANITA AL CAFFÈ CON PANNA MONTATA

Perhaps one of the most sought-after specialties, this is made from sweetened leftover coffee that is stored in the freezer. If you don't have any leftover sweetened espresso, use this recipe:

- 8 ounces sugar
- 2 pints water
- 4 ounces finely ground coffee
- 1 egg white, stiffly beaten

Put water and sugar in a saucepan and boil for a few minutes. Add the ground coffee to the sugar syrup and leave to infuse for ten minutes. Strain thoroughly through a fine sieve and cool. When cold, pour the syrup into a covered ice tray and put in the freezer. When partly frozen (about one-half hour), turn it into a bowl and beat in the stiffly beaten egg white and return to the ice tray. Freeze until firm and smooth, beating every half hour to break up the ice granules. An automatic ice cream maker does this even easier. Serve with whipped cream. Makes about four servings.

ICED COFFEE MILK SHAKE

- 1 pint milk
- 1 tablespoon coffee, brewed or instant
- 3 tablespoons sugar
- 6 ice cubes

Blend until frothy and serve immediately. Makes one serving.

FLAVORED COFFEES

I'm not a purist when it comes to flavored coffees. One of my favorite pastimes as a young adult was getting together with friends after work at the local saloon. That was where I first learned to toss a jigger of Kahlúa, a Mexican-style coffee liqueur, into a cup of coffee. I still enjoy that smooth taste in a darkly rich cup of coffee. Coffee drinks with liqueurs are delicious and fun.

Marc, a spirit from grape skins and pips, is commonly added to coffee served in the south of France, particularly Provence, and drunk as a recipe of equal parts of marc and coffee. The French have also given us the following liqueurs to lace coffee, usually in one-third amounts to two-thirds coffee: cognac, Armagnac, and the apple brandy of Normandy, calvados; crème de menthe, Cointreau, Benedictine, and crème de cacao.

Rum and the coffee liqueurs Tia Maria and Kahlúa are all great to add to coffee for an après dinner treat. Greeks use anise liqueurs like ouzo, the Belgians use pears, as in Poire, and the Swiss use a drink made from cherries, kirsch. Other fruit-flavored liqueurs, called *alcools blancs*, have been made from strawberries, raspberries, apricots, or plums, and go beautifully with coffee. Whiskey, more commonly used in coffee drunk in the British Isles, can be Scotch or Irish, or try American bourbon.

A twist of lemon or orange alongside an espresso adds a piquant bite that nicely balances the coffee's thick richness, and sweeteners from sugar to honey are traditional for some Turkish-style coffees.

None other than esteemed French cookbook author Simone Beck opted for the Ethiopian trick of adding salt to coffee. She swore that the flavor of coffee was enhanced if, at the moment of pouring boiling water over the coffee, one added a tiny pinch of salt. Moroccans use whole black peppercorns, some health-conscious Americans add honey or raw sugar instead of white granulated sugar, and a pinch of cinnamon powder or a stick of cinnamon is quite common in Italy.

Malt coffee has the addition of toasted barley. Freshly pounded saffron pistils and cardamom seeds give a delicate perfume to Turkish coffee made in Saudi Arabia, and in Mexico, brown sugar, cinnamon, and cloves are added for *café de olla*.

In Austria, a drink sometimes referred to as Viennese coffee employs dried figs to sweeten steaming hot cups of coffee; and in Belgium, land of *chocolat*, little squares of chocolate are placed along the saucers either to be eaten as you sip coffee or to be placed into the cup to melt and flavor the coffee.

The best of the above described "flavorings" are those which are fresh or, when fruited liqueurs are used, certainly those which are carefully and exquisitely made. My only criticism of flavored coffees is directed at the packaged brands on the grocer's shelves that mix coffee with nearly anything for a coffee drink; some work and others are a bit of a stretch. Some of the more popular flavorings are raspberry, vanilla, mint, cinnamon and cardamom, chocolate, amaretto, and such nut flavors as almond, macadamia, and hazelnut. On the label they sound fine, but further reading reveals these coffee drinks are usually made of a considerable list of synthetic ingredients.

It does seem a shame to take a fine handful of beautiful beans, roast them to perfection, and then bruise them, even if ever so slightly, with a contrasting flavor, particularly when those additional flavors are not in their natural state but are artificial flavorings with stabilizers, enhancers, and all the rest.

My conclusion regarding flavored coffees is that you should make your own, using fine fruit syrups, liqueurs, chocolate, or nut concentrates.

A Word About Cardamom

Cinnamon sticks are frequently served in Italian coffeehouses to use as stirrers, which gently imparts a delicate cinnamon taste to the coffee. Although Arab coffee is sometimes made with ground cinnamon thrown into the coffee while it is brewing, the cinnamon stick is not as common as it is in many places outside the Middle East. Another popular spice is the clove, usually added in whole cloves rather than the ground spice.

However, it is neither clove nor cinnamon that is the most popular flavoring in Arab countries but cardamom. This wonderfully fragrant spice is sometimes served as a condiment following the brewing process, but more frequently it is cooked along with the coffee as an integral ingredient to the rich, thick, syrupy Arab coffee.

Cardamom comes in two varieties: green and black, but the shades of green, from white to very dark, are many, and indicate the amount of processing that has been done to the pods. Dark green indicates that the pods have been heavily dried, usually in an oven; light green pods are usually dried in the air outside; and white is not at all a natural hue, but is a result of bleaching the old-fashioned way, with hydrogen peroxide; it is also the most expensive, probably because so many bakers like the fact that the whiteness blends in with the flours they use. Coffee drinkers should avoid the powders, or seeds, and opt for lush green pods; they add the truest flavor to the coffee without overwhelming it in any way.

Black cardamom, nearly one inch long, as compared to the green seeds, which are about one-quarter of an inch, are a botanical cousin but not truly cardamom. They are grown in Africa and dried in a style that lends a smoky taste to the seed, often referred to by connoisseurs as a peppery taste. It is this black cardamom that is common to food in Pakistan and northern India, particularly Indian *garam masala* spice mixes.

Cardamom comes in whole pods, decorticated (whole seeds), or ground up. Naturally, seeds and ground cardamom are considerably less expensive than the whole pods, which can cost upwards of seventy dollars per pound, but one sacrifices flavor by using the ground seed. Like all other expensive spices, particularly vanilla and saffron, the high price tag is a result of the extensive hand labor; cardamom pods must be picked before they are split open to expose the dark, slightly sticky seeds within. The pods grow at the root of the *Elettaria cardamomum*, which is a plant that grows usually eight to fifteen feet high among the shade of various tropical trees.

Cardamom is grown in Africa, primarily, but thrives most places near the equator: India (the world's largest producer), Sri Lanka, and only recently, Central America. Guatemala, which grows some of the finest cardamom in the world, has as its biggest market the Middle East, still the largest users of cardamom in coffee. The delicate floral taste is a nice addition to the acidic thick Arab-style coffee and is best used by itself in coffee, although some people can't leave well enough alone and add other spices.

Despite the high price, a little bit goes a long way. Cardamom pods have a long shelf life when properly stored tightly in glass jars and placed in a cool, dry area; good-quality cardamom is a worthy investment, and even the most ambitious baker or enthusiastic Arab coffee fiend can buy enough cardamom pods for a year for under ten dollars.

INSTANT AND OTHER PUTRIFICATIONS

I do believe that if you take fabulous beans, roast them to taste, and then freeze-dry them in a way that can avoid freezer burn, you could come up with a satisfying cup. It's just that I've never tasted one. Ironically, instant coffee seems to work well in cooking, but here, again, freshly brewed coffees make better-tasting coffee-flavored foods, whether they're desserts or main dishes.

DECAFFEINATED: THE GOOD, THE BAD, AND THE UGLY

My feelings are pretty much the same about decaffeination. If caffeine is truly a problem and you love the taste of coffee, then either drink espressos, which, despite their intensity, have less caffeine in them than traditionally brewed coffee, or opt for coffee-flavored foods like ice cream or candy.

While espresso generally does have less caffeine than regular coffee, a cautionary "usually" must be attached here. Theoretically, since espresso is made in smaller quantities of higher-quality beans, and with less water, lower tem-

Tune in on "Arthur Godfrey Time," CBS-TV and Radio, Monday through Friday.

peratures, and a shorter period of time, less caffeine ends up in the beverage, usually from 90 to 150 milligrams per cup.

Generally speaking, coffee has caffeine levels ranging from 60 to 180 milligrams per five-ounce serving of regular coffee, but much depends on the bean. Robusta coffees have twice as much caffeine as arabica coffee, probably another reason to choose only specialty coffees. The ratio of coffee to water in most brewing formulas, the conditions of time, temperature, and turbulence experienced by the grounds themselves, and the size of the actual coffee cup are all part of the equation.

To clarify all of this, understand that if you have a small espresso, you will definitely get less caffeine than in any other coffee drink; if you have a regular coffee, you will get less caffeine with arabica beans than with robusta beans, and, obviously, you will get less caffeine with coffee served in the traditional five- to six-ounce cup than a huge ten- to twelve-ounce mug. In other words, it pays to get the good stuff, drink it in moderate amounts, and savor it fully.

While I have mentioned that some of the water-filtered coffees, sometimes referred to as Swiss or European processed coffees, are good, most decaffeination requires more chemicals and nonfood items than you truly want to know about, and they simply mask or obliterate the better qualities of a good cup of coffee.

What to Do With the Spent Grounds

Spent coffee grounds should never be reused to make coffee, but they have other uses: great for your compost or to sprinkle around plants; and much has been substantiated with subsequent medical research on the benefits of coffee grounds as a deodorant, antiseptic, germicide, and bactericide. Perhaps the most common use for used grounds is the same as for spent tea leaves: to tell one's fortune, as noted earlier, but we suggest considering coffee as a design element in handmade paper.

Coffee Notes

This is a great way to recycle not only the spent grounds, but all those paper bags that you bring your coffee beans home in and all those endless items of mail that you normally throw out—with the following "recipe," you can turn them all into paper art!

DIRECTIONS

Shred paper until you get about six large handfuls. Put the paper in a pan large enough to accommodate an 8x10-inch frame, and add enough water so that there are about two inches of water on top of the paper. After soaking overnight, the paper should have become real mushy. Staple a fine screen (a window screen scrap is perfect) to a 5x7-inch or 8x10-inch wooden frame or discarded embroidery hoop.

To make your first sheet of paper, put the frame into the pan at a 45-degree angle and slide it under the mushy paper mixture. Then lift the frame straight up and, using a dull knife, scrape off enough of the mixture back into the pan so that you have a nice thin layer remaining on the screen.

Sprinkle a teaspoon or more of *dried* spent coffee grounds on top of the wet paper in whatever pattern you choose. Let the paper sheet dry, which should take about ten to twenty minutes. Carefully peel off the dried sheet and use it to make wrapping paper, stationery, placemats, lampshades, and anything else you could make with decorative handmade papers. Repeat the process until the mushy paper mixture is used up.

Coffee Trivia
To Perk You Up and Astonish Your Coffee-Loving Friends

— ◇◇◇ —

Now that you've skimmed this book, it's time to dazzle your close acquaintances and intimate friends, in and out of the coffeehouse. The following are trivia sure to please the diehard Scrabble or Jeopardy player, the superficially ignorant, and all those in between.

First one to memorize them all gets to buy everyone in the coffeehouse a nonfat double latte, hold the chocolate, add the cinnamon, don't forget the one ice cube and, please, put that in a porcelain cup, not a paper one with those ridiculous finger protection cardboards that only make it more difficult to hold on to your too hot coffee. Or, the coffee selection of your choice.

The Trivia, Please

More than eight species of coffee share the same general characteristics, but only three turn up in most coffee lovers' search for the Holy Grail (the Perfect Brew): arabica, robusta, and, occasionally, liberica.

Good things
happen
over coffee . . .

The bended knee
   may be out of date
And the high laced shoes
   may be gone of late;
But the boy and the girl
   and the coffee stay
As when Pop found Mom
   just yesterday.

For coffee is always
   on the scene . . .
Lending its warmth
   to each couple's dream,
And over some coffee,
   how often do
The dreams of the warmest
   hearts come true!

The finest coffees are made from the arabica beans, and all specialty coffees come from the arabica bean.

The coffee plant is native only to Ethiopia and Yemen.

Coffee has been transplanted successfully all over the world: in Java, Sumatra, and other islands of the former Netherlands Indies, in India, Africa, Latin America, and the West Indies.

Coffee contains a remarkably high quantity of niacin, about 10 percent of the U.S. recommended daily requirement per cup of coffee.

Overroasting or overextraction are the reasons behind the occasional appearance of oily droplets on the surface of brewed black coffee.

The brewing time for fine grind is one to four minutes; for drip grind, four to six minutes; for regular grind, six to eight minutes.

Coffee should be drunk at a temperature of 185 to 190 degrees Fahrenheit.

The only coffees grown commercially in the United States are Hawaiians, primarily Molokai and Kona.

About fifty varieties of coffee are available for ordinary commercial use.

Coffee futures are contracts bought and sold through the New York Coffee and Sugar Exchange. Actual coffee is rarely delivered against these contracts; futures are used mainly to protect price position (hedging).

Liberica is of such poor quality that hardly any coffee found in the United States contains it.

The small unassuming fruit of the coffee bean resembles a cherry and is the size of the end of your little finger.

The three parts of the bean include the outer casing; the inner gummy mass, called the pulp; and the inside green bean, usually two flat beans, but can be one small round bean, known as the peaberry.

Specialty coffees grow best in altitudes of 3,300 to 7,000 feet above sea level.

Coffee grows where warm temperature, abundant rain, bright sunshine, high altitude, and rich volcanic soil are present.

Most coffee is grown in latitudes between 25 degrees north and 25 degrees south of the equator.

Coffee is grown between the Tropic of Cancer and Tropic of Capricorn across the Americas, the Caribbean islands, to Africa, Arabia, the Malagasy Republic, India, and the East Indian and Pacific Islands in a total of more than sixty countries worldwide.

The coffee industry is second only to oil in the number of people it employs throughout the world: 25 million.

Specialty arabica coffee cherries need six to seven months to grow to maturity, two months longer than their cousins, robusta beans, which grow at lower levels.

A typical coffee tree produces only about two thousand cherries per year.

The coffee tree begins flowering in its third year.

The flowers of a coffee tree are white and bloom in clusters at the base of the leaves; they have a highly aromatic scent.

A coffee tree usually produces its first good crop of fruit in its fifth or sixth year.

Even on a single branch, one can find both ripe (red) and unripe (green) cherries, which is why all specialty coffees are still picked by hand.

It takes about five pounds of cherries to produce a single pound of green coffee beans.

The average specialty coffee tree produces one pound of green coffee beans *per year.*

When coffee cherries ripen, they mature into a bright shade of red, although in a few species they become yellow.

The chemical composition of coffee consists of three elements: caffeine (stimulant), caffeol (flavor and aromatic scent), and caffetannic acids (taste appeal).

Dry coffee beans are 25 percent carbohydrates, 35 percent relatively water-insoluble woody cellulose matter, 13 percent oils, 13 percent proteins, 4 percent ash, 8 percent acids, 1 percent trigonelline (nontoxic alkaloid), and 1 percent caffeine.

The amount of caffeine in the main types of coffee beans varies only slightly: robusta, liberica, and excelsa beans contain 2 to 4.5 percent caffeine, and arabica contains 1 to 1.7 percent caffeine.

A pound of coffee yields about forty cups of coffee.

Ten cups yield only eleven calories.

Plantation-grown coffee trees are kept pruned to an average of six feet and are usually planted in rows four to nine feet apart.

Wild coffee trees grow from fourteen to twenty feet tall.

Coffee trees have been known to bear fruit when over one hundred years old.

Plantation coffee trees usually live twenty-five to forty years, but are at their prime at ten to fifteen years.

Linnaeus was the first to give the coffee plant its Latin designation, *Coffea*, which is found in his *Genera Plantarum*, published in 1737. He was not its discoverer. Curator de Jussieu of the Amsterdam Conservatory named the coffee plant *Jasminum arabicum;* he got the *arabicum* right, but was wrong in thinking the plant a part of the jasmine family.

The coffee tree bears blossoms and berries at the same time, but at different stages of maturity, thus requiring frequent hand-picking of the same branch.

When Jamaican bats are heard sucking the ripe cherry pulp of the coffee tree, it is a sign to the farmer that the coffee harvest can begin.

Espresso, despite its stronger taste, generally has less caffeine per cup than a regular cup of coffee.

Every nation that has been exposed to coffee pronounces the word in a similar way; the exception is Armenia, whose language, Armenian, refers to coffee as *sourj.*

In the Middle East, women are not accepted in the coffeehouse; only men gather together there. This is as true today as it was five centuries ago. Only the most modern and sophisticated places in Istanbul, Damascus, and Cairo, catering primarily to tourists, admit women today.

San Francisco was the first point of entry for coffee for many years, thus making it one of the most outstanding centers for coffee in the United States.

A Glossary of Coffee Terms

The following includes both the obvious and the obscure facts that most coffee enthusiasts ask about at one time or another. Much of this information is an aside to the main text of this book, but is included here to help the buyer choose the bean from the pebble in the vast plethora of choices now available. The best thing you can do is find a coffee merchant of fine reputation, put your trust in her, and start your trek down the road to the "divine nectar." *Bon saveur!*

Abyssinian Abyssinia is the former name of Ethiopia, and the word Abyssinian is still used to refer to the gathered or wild coffees grown there.

acid A flavor component of coffee that comes in many varieties which do not taste the same, although to the uneducated palate they taste similar, e.g. lactic acid, malic acid, citric acid, and tartaric acid. Acid is the taste predominantly linked to naturally occurring acids like citric and malic. *See also* **sour.**

acidity Desirable cup characteristic; the wineyness of a smooth, rich cup with snap, life, and thinness. **Acidy** is the adjective form.

afloats Term for coffee enroute on ships to ports of destination.

after-dinner roast A dark brown roast of coffee with a bittersweet tang; also known as espresso roast.

altura "Heights" in Spanish. Describes Mexican coffee which has been high or mountain grown. Offers a light acidy brew.

American roasts Coffee roasted medium brown, to the North American taste; with dry surface, has a definite acidy snap.

Approved Coffee Measure (ACM) The proper proportion of water to coffee: two level tablespoons of ground coffee for every six ounces of water.

arabica, *Coffea arabica* Earliest cultivated species of coffee tree and still most widely grown. The best of the three types of coffee (others being robusta and liberica).

arabigo Coffee seed, different from Bourbon; it is a larger, flat type of bean considered better in quality and most suitable for higher altitudes.

aroma The term used for the odor of brewed coffee versus *bouquet*, which is used for the odor of the coffee grounds only. Some types of aromas include fruity, floral, malty, spicy, caramel- or syrup-like, and chocolaty.

baking Slow-roasting beans.

balance Tasting term for the state in which no single characteristic overwhelms others, but in which is displayed sufficient complexity to be interesting.

bale A package containing an amount of coffee known as a half, which weighs 80 kilos, or 175 pounds. Applied to Mocha or Harar coffee.

batch roaster Apparatus which roasts a given quantity or batch of coffee at a time.

belou Arabic for "sweet" (applied to the amount of sugar you want in your coffee, as opposed to *mazbout*, medium, or *murra*, unsweetened).

biggin A pot with a filter that is suspended in the mouth to hold the coffee grounds.

bitter A taste description of beans which are overly extracted, i.e., having too thin a liquor from too fine a grind. Dark roasts, while intentionally bitter, should taste hearty.

black beans Dead coffee beans that have dropped from trees before the harvest; the basic unit in grading imperfections in coffee on the New York Coffee Exchange.

bland This is a taste term which actually has two meanings: the taste of a cup that is made with too coarse a grind and underextracted liquor, resulting in an insipid flavor; or the taste of a low-grown coffee which is insipid no matter how much coffee is used.

blend Mixture of two or more straight coffees.

body The sense of heaviness, richness, or thickness when one tastes coffee that is full in the mouth. Some connoisseurs describe body as a syrupy, buttery feel, but the essence is a mouth-filling sensation.

bold A size classification of coffee beans—larger than medium but smaller than larger or extra large. Also, a generic reference to size, as in "sufficiently bold."

briny A taste description of coffee which has sat too long following brewing; it is actually a salty taste to some palates, but others perceive it as burnt.

broca Spanish for *Hemileia vastatrix*, or the dreaded bean borer.

bright Taste designation to describe a lively mouth "feel" of the coffee.

brown roast Coffee roasted to North American tastes: medium brown.

Bullhead "Monstrosity" in which the coffee bean develops to more than twice its normal size. Usually occurs when two beans grow together, and they usually break apart during roasting.

bunn Coffee beans or, specifically the kernel of the coffee bean as opposed to its husk (in Arabic, called *habb al-bunn*).

bunnu Arabic for the raw coffee bean.

café au lait French coffee drink with milk.

café bonifeur French West Indies term for coffee thoroughly cleaned and polished; named for the polishing machine in Guadeloupe.

café con leche Spanish or Portuguese dark roasted mixed with sugar and served with heated milk. Warm buttered bread is the classic accompaniment.

café de panno Portuguese term for coffee picked "in the cloth," a cotton sheet spread onto the ground under the coffee bean tree so that beans do not touch the ground.

café despolpadi Portuguese term for washed coffee or pulped coffee.

café macho Slang for the very highest class coffee in Latin American countries.

cafeate Nicaraguan term for coffee with milk.

cafezinho A method of preparing coffee in Colombia that is similar to the Costa Rican method which uses a flannel cloth folded up into a filter or "sock" into which coffee grounds are placed. Boiling water is then poured over the grounds. Makes a strong thick brew.

caffè latte Italian coffee drink with milk.

caffeine Alkaloidal substance in the coffee bean and coffee leaf; average caffeine content of green coffee is about 1.5 percent.

caracol Spanish for "peaberry"; also the term used for the separation of firsts and seconds of the peaberry bean.

caracolilo Spanish for "small peaberry"; most popular type of Dominican coffee.

carangola Natural hybrid of coffee found in the Carangola District of Minas Gerais, Brazil.

cezva Triangular, open-mouthed boiler with a broad base, used for making Turkish coffee; called a *dezva* in Serbo-Croatian.

cherry The ripe fruit of the coffee tree. The seeds, with coverings removed, become green coffee.

chicory Used as filler in coffee. The raw root of the *Cichorium intybus* plant is cut into slices, kiln-dried, and then roasted in the same manner as coffee, then ground into a powder and used as an additive to coffee; very common and popular in Louisiana.

chop Each invoice of coffee is made up into a number of divisions called chops. The bags in each division are marked with their own particular chop number before being shipped from the country of production to their various destinations.

cinnamon roast Coffee roasted slightly lighter than the North American norm.

city roast Term for New York City medium-dark-roasted coffee; not as dark as full city roast.

coffea arabica Latin botanical name for arabica beans, the best coffee beans grown.

coffea canephora Latin botanical name for robusta beans, a lower grade of coffee but the type most commonly produced.

coffea excelsa Latin botanical name for excelsa beans, a lower grade of coffee.

coffea liberica Latin botanical name for liberica beans, a lower grade of coffee.

coffee "The seed of cultivated varieties of *Coffea arabica, C. liberica, and C. robusta,*" according to the U.S. Department of Agriculture.

coffee grader An official, licensed by the Coffee Exchange, who grades coffee according to types recognized by the Exchange.

coffeol, coffee oil, coffee essence Volatile, oily substance developed in the coffee bean during roasting.

continental roast Coffee roasted dark brown, with a bittersweet tang.

continuous roaster Large commercial coffee-roasting apparatus which roasts coffee continuously, rather than in batches.

cupping Process that professional tasters use to taste the bean in the cup. It is a taste, savor, and spit process, usually with a brew that is at room temperature or colder.

dark French roast Coffee roasted nearly black.

dark roast Coffee roasted darker than the North American norm.

decaffeinated or caffeine-free coffee Coffee roasted from whole beans which have had their caffeine removed during the green bean state.

decortication Removing the parchment skin from the coffee bean.

dellel or della A pot with a long, thin spout for pouring coffee. Sometimes known as a Baghdad boiler; common in Syria.

demitasse "Half cup," in French; it is a half-size or three-ounce cup.

drip method Brewing coffee by allowing hot water to settle down through a bed of ground coffee.

dry fermenting Process used to ferment washed coffee, without water.

dry roast Roasting process in which no water is used to check the roast; the operator depends solely on his cooling apparatus to check it.

earthy A taste designation "of the earth" for low-grade or "dirty" coffee made with poor processing methods such as drying beans on the ground, or a positive designation for beans that are tangy or spicy, such as those from Indonesia.

elephant A size designation for gigantic coffee beans.

ensacador: Portuguese word for "coffee bagger."

espresso A roast of coffee and a method of brewing using the darkest roasts and finest grounds to produce a very strong, rich cup.

European preparation A term sometimes used to describe coffee from which imperfect beans, pebbles, and other foreign matter have been removed by hand.

European roast Coffee roasted dark brown, with a bittersweet tang.

excelso Comprehensive grade of Colombian coffee consisting of qualities corresponding to supremo and extra types; may include peaberries of those types.

exotic A taste description for coffees which are described as sweet and spicy, for example, those from East Africa and Indonesia. Used to describe both aroma and flavor that are unexpected or unusual.

extra fine Best grade of Venezuelan coffee.

fazenda A Brazilian coffee plantation. They number about 230,000 and produce nearly 30 million bags of coffee, about one-third of the world's crop, primarily robusta beans.

fermenting A step in the preparation of ripe coffee, consisting of putting pulped coffee into tanks with or without water. This process can take hours to days, depending on altitude and temperature.

Filter method Brewing coffee by any method in which water filters down through a bed of ground coffee.

finca Spanish for "farm"; a coffee plantation which is smaller than the hacienda of Guatemala and the *fazenda* of Brazil.

fines The very finest particles of ground coffee.

finjan Cup for Turkish coffee.

flatbean Santos A larger bean without the curly characteristics generally associated with Bourbon Santos. This bean is usually void of acid.

flavor Tasting term used to describe the combination of acidity, aroma, and body in a cup of coffee. Also used to describe specific flavor characteristics, e.g., malty, herbal, spicy, et al.

fluidized bed roaster A machine that roasts coffee by elevating the beans in a stream of very hot air.

French roast Coffee roasted dark brown, at times nearly black, with a bittersweet tang, and roasted high enough to bring the natural oil of the coffee to the surface of the bean.

full city roast Term for New York coffee indicating a roast slightly heavier than a city roast; beans are roasted to their full development.

futures Purchase or sale of coffee or other commodity contracts for delivery in the future. Contracts are bought and sold like stocks; opposite of spot.

glazing Roasted coffees are sometimes glazed to preserve their natural flavor and aroma. Common in the southern states of the U.S. The word *coating* is also used to designate the same process.

Good Hard Bean A grade of Costa Rican coffee grown at altitudes of 3,300 to 3,900 feet.

goute-café Specially shaped spoon with a deep round bowl for professional coffee tasting of brewed and espresso coffees, similar to the *taste-vin* of the sommelier (wine taster).

green coffee Unroasted coffee.

groundy Having earthy taste sometimes found in damaged coffees; different from mustiness, which may contain actual mold.

hacienda Spanish for "farm" or "ranch"; in Venezuela it means "coffee plantation." These are larger than the *fincas* of Guatemala but smaller than the *fazendas* of Brazil

hard Trade term for low-quality coffee.

hard bean High-grade, mountain-grown coffee from Central or South America, where the cool mountain temperatures produce a slowly matured, dense bean. Also grades of both Guatemalan and Costa Rican coffee.

harsh Term for a certain coffee flavor; Rio coffees are deemed harsh.

hidy Description of coffee that smells like hides because the odor can actually come from contact with hides.

heavy roast Very dark-roasted coffee with a bittersweet tang.

high grown *Arabica* coffees grown at altitudes over 2,000 feet, and usually higher. Superior to coffees grown at lower altitudes. *High grown* also applies to many grade descriptions.

high roast Coffee roasted slightly darker than North American norm.

hopper Cooling vat for freshly roasted beans which uses a mechanical stirrer to move the beans around and cool them down; timing varies with each roaster, as does temperature to cool the beans.

hulling Last step before milling in the preparation of washed coffee. Operation is done by machines that remove the parchment and silver skin.

husk In Arabic, *al-qahwa al-qishriya*; the outside of the berry or the *qishr* (*kishr*).

husking Cleaning coffee beans that have been dried in the cherry. Coffee is said to be "in the husk" when the whole fruit is dried without water.

ibrik *or* **ibriq** Traditional open-mouthed coffeepot or vessel designed for easy pouring, i.e., a pitcher or ewer, most often with a long handle, used to make Turkish coffee; in Turkey, the pot is called *cezve*, and it is usually tinned brass or copper; in Greece it is called a *birki*.

imperfections black beans, broken beans, shells, immatures, quakers, stones, and pods—imperfections in the sample that affect the way a coffee is graded.

instant coffee Soluble coffee, a convenience food made by rapidly dehydrating freshly brewed coffee; reconstituted by adding boiling water.

Italian roast Term for coffee sometimes roasted darker than French, with a bittersweet taste and large amounts of oil on the surface, used extensively in Italy and many other coffee-producing countries. Typical choice for espresso and *caffe lattes*.

ixicara Portuguese for "cup of mocha."

kafa Ethiopian coffee that grows wild; also the word for "coffee" in Bosnia and Herzegovina.

kafana Coffeehouse in Bosnia and Herzegovina.

Kaffa The homophonically named region in southwest Ethiopia that some believe to be the probable source of the word "coffee," but in actuality the word "coffee" comes from the Arabic, *qahweh*, meaning wine, coffee, or any drink made from a plant.

Kaffekränzchen Social meetings at private homes in Germany during the sixteenth and seventeenth centuries at which people played games and cards and listened to music.

kahveci A person skilled in the art of preparing Turkish coffee.

kahveh Turkish word which refers to the beverage, not the plant.

k'hawah Arabic for coffee (also transliterated as *qahwah* and *qahweh*).

kanaka An *ibrik* (also spelled *tanaka*).

kofftafel "Coffee table" in Dutch; a noontime meal of coffee with sandwiches or a hot dish.

koppchen Bowls or handleless cups made of silver, pewter, pottery or faience from which seventeenth-century coffee drinkers would sip their brew.

kernel The part of the fruit of the coffee bean known in Arabic as the bunn or *habb al-bunniya* or *al-qahwa al-bunniya*.

kiraathane Reading room; neighborhood coffeehouse in Turkey; also a teahouse in Turkey.

kishr A drink resulting from the boiled, toasted flesh of the coffee cherry.

liberica (*Coffea liberica*) A species native to Liberia, Africa, formerly mixed to some extent with Bourbon Santos but considered to be of a low grade.

light French roast Coffee roasted slightly darker than the North American norm.

light roast Coffee roasted lighter than the North American norm.

Longberry Harar Grade of coffee produced in Ethiopia falling between the all-long bean and the inferior all-short bean.

MAM Acronym for Medellin, Armenia, and Manizales, three of the most famous and best coffees of Colombia.

mancalah *or* **manqala** An easy-to-learn, fast-playing game using twelve to fourteen hemispherical hollow pieces or stones played on a game board, very commonly played in coffeehouses in the Near East from the earliest of times, and very common in Africa. Gaining popularity as a game for children in the United States.

marqaha Coffee euphoria; a sixteenth-century peninsular Arabic term describing the physical and mental effects of coffee; most probably from the Ethiopian.

mazagran French drink composed of cold coffee and seltzer water; the original iced coffee drink.

mazbout "Medium sweet," in Arabic; *belou* means "sweet," *murra* means "unsweetened."

medium roast, medium high roast Coffee roasted to standard North American tastes; medium brown.

Melior or plunger-type brewer Melior is the brand name of a popular French brewer which separates spent grounds by forcing a filter down through the coffee. Also known as the plunge pot.

mellow Tasting term used for a coffee that's middle-of-the-road, having a balanced flavor that's not too acidy and not too syrupy.

Middle Eastern "Turkish" coffee ground to a powder, sweetened, brought to a boil, and served, grounds and all.

mild Trade term for high-quality arabica coffees, used to describe coffees produced in countries other than Brazil. Often contrasted with hard or inferior coffees. Formerly used to indicate those free from the harsh Rio flavor. It has also come to mean a coffee that is delicate in flavor yet not bland.

murra "Unsweetened" in Arabic; *mazbout* is "medium sweet"; *belou* is "sweet."

musty Flavor in coffee that either has been overheated or lacked proper drying or aging. Mustiness is generally undesirable, although mustiness of age is very desirable by some.

nargileh Turkish water pipe for smoking tobacco or hashish, commonly passed around a coffeehouse.

OID *Oost Indische Bereiding*, Dutch for "East Indies method," which consists of letting beans dry before splitting and removing the bean from the husk.

open pot coffee Perfect for campers, outdoorsy people, and purists of a sort, the open pot is used to make coffee by steeping fine-ground coffee two to four minutes, then straining through cheesecloth (if you're a purist). Pouring some cold water over the surface will force the coffee grounds to sink to the bottom of the pot. Radicals put the shell of one egg into the pot on the belief that they will absorb some of the cloud-forming sediment of the brew.

parchment One of the three skins of the coffee fruit, known as the endocarp, it lies between the flesh or outer skin and the pulp and the innermost silver skin, and is removed during the hulling process.

peaberry Rounded small bean from an occasional coffee cherry that contains only one seed instead of the usual flat-sided pair. This is a result of the nondevelopment of one of the ovules, an abortion most common among arabica trees. It is light tan to greenish and the size of a pea.

penny universities The name given to London's coffeehouses because for pennies, one could sit among the learned men of letters and arts of the day and learn, all the while drinking one's precious coffee.

percolation Any method of brewing coffee in which the hot water filters down through a bed of ground coffee (percolates), but more frequently referring to the actual coffeemaker which uses the force of bubbles in boiling water to draw water up a tube and over the ground coffee.

pergamino *See* **parchment.**

points Term used by coffee graders to designate differences in grades. The Coffee Exchange operators also use this term to indicate the fluctuations in prices where one hundred points equals one cent, U.S.

pulping First step when using the wet method. After picking, machines are used to rub away the outer skin with friction without crushing the beans.

pyrolysis The chemical decomposition of the fats and carbohydrates of the raw bean into the delicate oils, resulting in the acute aroma and flavor we know as "that coffee smell."

qahveh khaneh "Schools of wisdom," what the first coffeehouses in Constantinople (Istanbul) were called, because they were the meeting places for men of the arts and literature of the day.

qahwah Arabic for "coffee"; the stimulating beverage made from the fruit of the *Caffea arabica.*

qahwah bunniya The beverage made from the kernels of the fruit (*bunn*) alone or from the husks and kernels together.

qahwah qishriya The beverage made exclusively from the husks (*see* **kishr**).

qat The shrub *catha eduis*, also known as *kafta* or *kat*, whose stimulating leaves were chewed for their mildly narcotic effect; still used extensively in Yemen.

qishr *See* **kishr.**

quakers Coffee beans which are blighted, unripened, undeveloped, discolored, or deformed; does not usually affect flavor if a few get by, but a number of them will lessen the quality of the flavor considerably. They appear much less often in washed coffee beans.

raw coffee Seeds of the coffee cherry after fermentation and separation from the outer skins.

regular roast Term for medium brown roast of coffee roasted to North American tastes.

Rio coffee Bitter, medicinal-tasting coffee popular in the Balkans, Yugoslavia, and Greece.

Rio flavor Heavy and harsh taste, sometimes present in even fancy mild coffees. One of those characteristics which you either love or hate; often referred to as a medicinal taste.

Rio smell An odor found in coffee with trichloroanisole. The smell of trichloroanisole is noticeable even in quantities as small as 1 part per 100 milliards.

Rioy Iodinelike, medicinal flavor in processed coffee beans which are mass harvested. It is a variation of the Brazilian coffee, Rio, and its harsh flavor was often counteracted by chicory for New Orleans-style roasts.

roast The heating of beans to a certain style of flavor which results in certain styles of density of flavor, from light to dark.

robusta (*Coffea robusta* or Coffea canephora) Botanical species of the genus *Coffea*, whose only true competitor is *Coffea arabica*. It is inferior and lacks arabica's aroma; most commonly used in instant coffees.

rubbery Coffee master term for the taste of robusta beans.

Rubiaceae Botanical family to which coffee belongs.

Self-drinker Coffee from a single place or country which is drunk without blending with other coffees or additives.

selo Villages in Bosnia and Herzegovina, where *kafa*, a "Turkish-style" coffee, is very popular.

Shortberry Harar Grade designation for Ethiopian coffee indicating a smaller bean than the Longberry Harar or the peaberry-sized Mocha.

silver skin Thin, papery covering on the coffee bean, located inside the parchment. One of several layers which must be removed either by the wet or dry method to reveal the bean.

sizing Grading of green beans by size, usually done by machines that can separate and distribute the different-sized beans. Principal grades in order from largest to smallest are triage, third flats, second flats, first flats, first peaberry, and second peaberry.

skimmings Any part of a bag of coffee that has been damaged in shipping by contact with moisture. The damaged portion is "skimmed off" and classified as either poor skimmings (P.S.), medium skimmings (M.S.), or good skimmings (G.S.).

soft A designation used for a low-acid green coffee that is of good drinking quality without any unpleasant taste characteristics; could be likened to *mellow*.

sorting Use of electronic color-sensitive machinery to eliminate all beans that are either lighter or darker than the standard to obtain coffee of top quality. Standards vary from company to company and from country to country.

sour A taste designation particularly linked to bacterial fermentation, the same process that produces lactic acid from lactose and acetic acid from alcohol. Sour-tasting beans are undesirable and come mostly from fermented green beans and processing errors. *Acid*, although sometimes used interchangeably with the word *sour*, is a desirable characteristic and is found in the bean. (*See* acid.)

Spanish roast Coffee with a bittersweet tangy taste, roasted dark brown.

specialty coffee Custom whole-bean coffees sold by country of origin, style of roast, or grades, sometimes with additional flavorings.

spicy A taste designation that refers to the aroma of a coffee versus its taste; some descriptions might be "peppery," "spicy," or reminiscent of some particularly sweet-smelling spice, e.g., cardamom, even though the actual spice may not be in the coffee.

spot Opposite of futures. Importers, brokers, jobbers, and roasters deal in actual coffee in warehouses or in the consuming countries.

straight coffee Unblended coffee from a single crop, region or country, and so designated and named.

Strictly Hard Bean (SHB) Highest grade of Guatemalan and Costa Rican coffees, indicating coffees grown at altitudes of 4,500 feet or higher; as opposed to Hard Bean (HB), which are grown between 4,000 and 4,500 feet.

Strictly High Grown Highest grade of El Salvadoran coffee, perhaps a misnomer since this is a very mild, undistinguished coffee at best.

Strictly High Grown Washed Highest of many grades of Haitian coffees, with mellow sweetness, fair body and acidity, and soft, rich flavor. Second best is High Grown Washed.

strong A taste designation used to refer to dark-roasted beans that are strong or "assertive," although it can reflect the presence of defects in the bean. It is incorrect to use this term to describe a coffee with a lot of caffeine, as, ironically, the lower-quality robusta coffees have a higher caffeine content than the arabica beans.

style Term used to designate the appearance of a whole coffee bean, whether roasted or green; a grade term.

sukar ziada *See* **below.**

summer roast Lighter roast used to prevent sweating caused by increased temperatures during the summer.

supremo Finest grade of Colombian coffee, a classic without extremes, full bodied but less so than Sumatran. Sometimes sold as supremo excelso, a combination of different grades (extra and supremo) or of caracolo and two grades of peaberry beans.

sweepings All loose coffee that is swept up from the ship's holds and the floors of the piers, including the beans in contact with the dirt on unclean floors. Sweepings are not to be removed from the piers for entry in the country but must be placed in containers by the steamship company or its agent and held for disposal or dumping. Coffee sweepings originating in and shipped from foreign countries are denied entry, and reconditioning is not permitted. They may be exported upon application to customs authorities.

sweet Trade term to describe coffee that tastes unharsh or undamaged in any way as opposed to the harshness of a Rio.

tangy A taste designation to indicate a wineyness or acidic fruitiness that is quite pleasantly sharp; most evident in high-grown Costa Rican coffees.

tannin The solid, yellowish white, astringent compound known as tannic acid constitutes about 8 percent of green coffee; roasting reduces it to about 4 percent. Provides the bite of coffee flavor.

tinto Coffee in Colombia or Brazil.

tipping When intense heat is applied too quickly during the roasting process, it results in charring the little germ or tip at the end of the coffee bean.

triage: French word used to describe broken beans; method of processing used in Haiti; and most recently, a grading term to designate the largest beans.

Turkish coffee Term both for the finely ground dark roast coffee famous in Turkey and for the style of preparation favored in the Middle East, most commonly using an *ibrik*, or long-handled open pot of brass or copper.

unwashed coffee Green coffee developed by the dry process which dries the entire fruit, removing the parchment and silver skin by hulling operations. Sometimes involves air-drying outside, with the beans spread out over the ground, and workers raking through the beans to turn them over, insuring that the bean will be dried evenly.

vacuum method Process in which a two-section coffeemaker sucks up the water, as a vacuum cleaner would, through the grounds; makes a clear, clean cup of coffee.

Viennese Designation for either the roast (slightly darker) or blend (two-thirds regular roast and one-third dark roast beans). Also the name of a coffee drink topped with whipped cream or black coffee with dried figs added for sweetness.

vintage Aged green unroasted coffee beans.

washed coffee Coffee prepared by the wet method, which involves removing the skin and pulp from the coffee bean while the berry is still moist and before it is dried.

whole bean Coffees which are processed (roasted) but not yet ground.

wild Taste designation to describe a coffee with extremes in aroma or flavor that could be called defects or attributes, e.g., Ethiopia Harar.

winey A taste designation for coffee with a fruity acid and smooth body, not unlike a fine red wine; Kenyan AA is a classic example of a winey coffee.

WIP *West Indische Bereiding* (Dutch for "West Indies method"), a process still used in Java, where the berries are stoned after harvesting to remove the beans from the skin and pulp, thus accelerating the drying process. Sometimes referred to as West Indian Preparation, a reference to coffee washed on-site on the plantation.

woody Green coffee which has lost is commercial value from deterioration.

zarf Ornamental metal holder for the handleless coffee cup used in the Levant, lands bordering the eastern shores of the Mediterranean and Aegean seas.

BIBLIOGRAPHY

Some of the older books listed here are out of print, but all can be found at major libraries.

Bersten, Ian, B. *Coffee Floats Tea Sinks, Through History and Technology to a Complete Understanding.* Sydney, Australia: Helion Books, 1993.

Bramah, Edward. *Tea & Coffee: A Modern View of Three Hundred Years of Tradition.* London: Hutchinson & Co., 1972.

Calvert, Catherine. *Coffee: The Essential Guide to the Essential Bean,* recipes by Jane Stacey. New York: Hearst Books, 1994.

Coffee Brewing Center of the Pan American Coffee Bureau, *CBC Coffee Workshop Manual.* New York, 1974.

Davids, Kenneth. *Coffee: A Guide to Buying, Brewing, and Enjoying,* San Francisco: 101 Productions, 1976.

DeMers, John. *The Community Kitchens Complete Guide to Gourmet Coffee.* New York: Simon and Schuster, 1986.

deLorme, Diane. *Coffee Cuisine.* New York: Macmillan, Artists & Writers Publications, 1972.

Hattox, Ralph S. *Coffee and Coffeehouses: The Origins of a Social Beverage in the Medieval Near East.* Seattle: University of Washington Press, 1985.

Heise, Ulla. *Coffee and Coffee-Houses,* trans. by Paul Roper from the German. Berlin: Schiffer Publishing Ltd., 1987.

Illy, Francesco, and Illy, Ricardo. *The Book of Coffee, A Gourmet's Guide,* New York: Abbeville Press, 1992.

Kummer, Corby. *The Joy of Coffee: The Essential Guide to Buying, Brewing, and Enjoying,* Shelburne, VT: Chapters Publishing, 1995.

Roden, Claudia. *Coffee.* New York: Penguin Books, 1981.

Schaefer, Charles and Violet. *Coffee: A Connoisseur's View of Coffee.* San Francisco: Yerba Buena Press, 1976.

Svicarovich, John; Winter, Stephen; and Ferguson, Jeff. *The Coffee Book, A Connoisseur's Guide to Gourmet Coffee,* New York: Prentice-Hall, Inc., 1976.

ACKNOWLEDGMENTS

Many wonderful coffee lovers and people in the coffee industry shared their research, acumen, and coffee moments with me. I cannot begin to acknowledge them for their efforts, but to all thank you, thank you, thank you. Of course, all responsibility for accuracy rests with me.

In particular, I want to offer many thanks to Sandra Tolchin and Larry L. Gorchow of Great American Coffee and Tea Company for selections from their extensive coffee paper ephemera collection; to Ralph Hattox, author of *Coffee and Coffee Houses*, and professor of Near East studies in the history department of Hampdon/Sidney College in Hampdon City, Virginia, to the Specialty Coffee Association of America, in Long Beach, California and Annemarie Grieve for her illustrations.

Thanks, many times, to the helpful staff at the Sausalito Public Library and to the many exceptional specialty coffee roasters who took the time to talk to, debate with, inform, and enchant me about favorite cups, trends, history, and how to best educate the consumer.

I am also grateful to Ian Bersten, B. Com. (ECS), author of *Coffee Floats, Tea Sinks*; Bob Gard of Majestic Coffee & Tea, Inc., of San Carlos, California; Byron Goo of Rainbow Caffe, Waipahu, Hawaii; Paul Katzeff and Jan Enos of Thanksgiving Coffee Company, Fort Bragg, California; Brooke McDonald and Helen Russell of Equator Coffee and Tea, San Rafael, California; Mike Mountanos, Ric Martin, and Diane Tortolano of Mountanos Brothers Coffee, South San Francisco, California; Jim Reynolds of Peet's Coffee and Tea, Berkeley, California; Ric Rhinehart of Cafe au Lait, Carson City, California; Augie Techeira of Freed, Teller & Freed's, San Francisco, California; recipe contributors Karen Strange, Gary Stotsky, and Diane Robbins; and all the many friends who contributed stories about their favorite cup: Miss D. of Sausalito, Doris Knapp, Diane Kordick, Virginia Williams Lusk, Richard-Thomas, and Amy Ulmer.

To my biggest fans and supporters, heartfelt thanks for your continuing enthusiasm and encouragement: Karen Benke, Suellen Bilow, Annemarie Grieve, William E. Johnston Jr., Sandy Parry, plus all my other friends for their voices of encouragement.

Many thanks to Carol Publishing Group and to the careful and considerate editing by Margaret Wolf and Deborah Dwyer, and to those amazing geniuses who developed overnight mail delivery, the word processing concept, the fax, e-mail, and other time-saving, hair-raising, magical, and maddening gadgets and techniques for today's writer.

Index